M000213778

"This is a message of grea[...] and those of us who strug[...] the pa[...] and aloneness of this planet. Frances Vaughan tells us what we most need to know — that love is what connects us to each other and to All, and love is what we come here to learn. This is a book to set your course by, to use as a touch-stone, and give you peace as you transition to the greater reality. Beautiful and *life*-saving."

Matthew McKay, Ph.D., author, *Seeking Jordan: How I Learned About Death and the Invisible Universe*

"I feel that *Seven Questions* will be a valuable contribution to the 'life after life' field. It is fairly short, easy to read, practical, reassuring, and written from the heart. This book arises from a deep and enduring friendship which continues whether or not the individuals are physically or nonphysically focused. I will undoubtedly be loaning this book to those who can be uplifted by it."

Ellen Jones-Walker, Monroe Institute Residential Trainer

"WOW! This writing/channeling will touch so many who are seeking to know that their loved ones remain close at hand and continue to communicate with us even after death. *Seven Questions* will open a lot of doors and windows for those who are ready to feel the wind of possibilities blowing in."

Regina Ochoa, medium who works with the Foundation for Mind-Being Research in Los Altos, CA

"*Seven Questions About Life after Life* is an accessible, vibrant, and fascinating look at what consciousness is. The wisdom of the channeled information from Frances calls for several re-readings and comes through with intensity, poignancy, and recognition of truth. I strongly recommend this book for anyone who wishes to engage in a deep reflection into who we are and what we someday will become, and for those who ache to actively interact with these ideas."

Lisa Smartt, author, *Words at the Threshold*, *Veil*, and *Cante Bardo*; Founder, The Final Words Project; Co-founder, The University of Heaven

Seven Questions
About Life After Life

BOOK ONE
The Greater Reality Series

Cynthia Spring and Frances Vaughan

Wisdom Circles Publishing

Wisdom Circles Publishing
1063 Leneve Place
El Cerrito, CA 94530
www.cindyspring.com
wave@cindyspring.com

For complete list of permissions for quoted material, please see "Permissions" (p. 151)

Cover graphic: Getty Images

Typesetting and Design: Margaret Copeland, Terragrafix
www.terragrafix.com

Publishing Consultant: Naomi Rose
www.naomirose.net

Proofreading: Gabriel Steinfeld, gstein@sonic.net

Author photograph: Stu Selland

BISAC: Afterlife and Reincarnation/Parapsychology/ESP

Printed in the United States of America

First printing 2019

ISBN: 978-09996989-1-4

Dedicated to all those who have ventured past the portals of normal consciousness to explore "the greater reality"

✳

I asked Frances: What will people think of me when I publish a channeled book?

She answered: Some will think you saintly, some ridiculous. You are neither.

CONTENTS

To My Collaborator

Hello Frances. After a dozen years of our friendship, and then your passing to a greater reality in the fall of 2017, you have returned. We've become collaborators on a book that we had talked about once or twice, but never began. I had no idea at the time that our book would take this form — "automatic writing," or a book channeled from one dimension to another.

In January 2018 I was moved to sit with a blank pad, wearing one of your blue scarves, and had a framed picture of your beautiful, smiling face. I lit a candle in front of me and began the exercise by calling on you. You showed up as if you were waiting for me to hear your call. I now believe it was *you* who were calling *me*. The words from you came as whole thoughts. I could barely keep up with the writing.

After a couple of sessions where we established a channel for communication, we met regularly and began an ongoing dialogue. The primary purpose was to create a short book that would open a door to an expanded consciousness for me and others. You said many such books are being written now between an incarnate person, in this case me, and someone who could now speak from the balcony of greater awareness. I am so grateful you chose to work with me.

We had conversations once or twice a week, and I wrote down our words. Our conversations flowed so easily that I kept forgetting that I'm in a space/time dimension of dense matter, and you're in a different reality with no physical location and no linear time. You said there was an urgency to getting this material out because of "upcoming upheavals" that would soon be upon the physical space/time world that I live in. You said the singular message would be helpful to many:

Death is a transition from one kind of life to another. Or as Bengali poet Rabindranath Tagore put more poetically:

> *Death is not extinguishing the light;*
> *it is putting out the lamp because dawn has come.*

To Our Readers

Welcome, dear reader. Who are you and why have you come to read this book? We hope to help you answer those questions. On the question of who you are, we'll be assisting you in what is a lifelong search that every person has. We can help answer the second question: you may be a person for whom the old order of pat answers to spiritual questions has fallen into disrepair. Or you may be a person who's heard about "channeled" books and wants to know more. Or you may have heard about an emerging form of spirituality that relies on direct experience. We're calling this an awareness of "a greater reality." For one reason or another, you're curious.

Frances and I have collaborated from different sides of the veil to offer you a glimpse of that greater awareness. You will also be an active participant, having your own insights and your own unique experience of what we will describe in simple and metaphorical terms. But words are words. Would you prefer to eat a menu with the words "grilled cheese sandwich with small salad and fries" or the real items? We'll suggest some real experiences for you to try along the way. Don't take our word for the existence of what we'll describe as our experiences, or descriptions from others who have mapped their versions of a greater reality. Nothing like going there yourself, and we'll provide portals for the journey.

So, Welcome! You'll find no dogma here, no fully formed map of "the new consciousness." This book is about a consciousness that is evolving, unfolding, and in which we're all participating — collaboratively and creatively as unique individuals. It's part magic carpet ride, and it's part labor-intensive demolition of the hypnotic programming of materialism we've all inherited. Letting go of pat answers means opening the door to genuine inquiry. Is spirituality all a delusion, or is there a reality to "soul" and "spirit?" It's entirely up to you how you incorporate what you find here into your everyday life. If this channeled book opens a door of inquiry for you, then you are ready to explore an expanded way of understanding reality.

Who We Are

Frances Vaughan and I met through mutual friends around 2006. At that time she was a practicing psychotherapist, past president of the Association for Transpersonal Psychology and had authored or co-authored several books. My husband, Charles Garfield, and Frances were colleagues in an ongoing program called *Metta Institute*. It provided in-depth workshops on spirituality for professional caregivers who were working with people in their dying time.

I've had a background as a media producer and for about 20 years I was deeply involved in local ecology in the San Francisco Bay Area. I've co-authored two other books and recently authored *The Wave and The Drop: Wisdom Stories about Death and Afterlife*. As that book was going through the last phases of typesetting and preparation for distribution, Frances and I began this collaboration. (Remember that she had died about four months earlier.) After a couple of sessions where we agreed on our purpose and established a format for the transmission, we have met regularly. I've chosen to use my given name, Cynthia, for authorship of this book. With friends I'm known as Cindy.

Both Frances and I are indebted to the channeling, writing, and research of many other explorers. This book's title harkens back to the book *Life After Life*, by Dr. Raymond

Moody, Jr., published in 1975. Dr. Moody is a psychiatrist and philosopher who was one of the first to study people who had been declared clinically dead but who came back to life with stories of visiting miraculous places filled with Love and Light. He coined the term "near-death experience" (NDE) that is widely used today.

During the late 1960s and 1970s, there sprang up all over the United States individuals and small groups studying NDEs, expanded psychic abilities, and children's stories of reincarnation. Mediums and psychics began receiving messages from "the other side" that became books. The consistent discovery in all these areas of endeavor was: reality is much larger and more complex than we ever imagined. Frances and I are adding this book to that lineage.

INTRODUCTION

For decades I had a pat answer to the question: *Is there an afterlife?* My answer was: I don't know. When I was forced to do some inquiry, I entered a world that I came to call "a greater reality." I can see in retrospect that I wouldn't have been moved to explore and consider this greater reality if I hadn't already been waking up to it. The catalyst was a conversation that I had with my mother-in-law during her hospice time. She asked me, "What happens when you die?" Instead of "I don't know," I told her a story that came out of the Hindu tradition called "The Wave and The Drop." I saw firsthand how much that story helped her across the threshold of death. And that led me to search for more answers from other traditions, ancient and contemporary. I ended up writing an entire book about the journey I took titled *The Wave and The Drop*.

I am aware of several dozen channeled books. I'm sure there are hundreds. Some say that the Jewish Old Testament, the Christian New Testament, and the Islamic Qur'an are all channeled. As Frances once said to me, "There is no such thing as an individually authored book. They're all channeled to a greater or lesser extent." Most of the contemporary channeled books are presented in the same chronological order in which they were received. A few are presented as material around a topic, and that is how I've chosen to organize this one.

Over the course of the automatic writing period, some key questions emerged. I chose to cluster Frances's answers to them. Early on, I was often assailed by doubts, as are most people who do automatic writing. "Where is this coming from?" "Am I making this up?" The personal exchanges within the writing sessions helped convince me this was truly Frances.

1

Don't Confine Yourself to a Limited Dimension

Very few of us remember our attempts to go from crawling along the floor to walking upright. What compelled us to keep trying even though we fell down so many times? We were going from one level of reality — *the floor* — to a greater reality — *freedom to move around as we like*. It took time, fortitude, and patience. But the drive to walk on two legs was innate, wired in.

So is the drive to expand our consciousness. We can't help but be aware of the greater freedom outside of religious or cultural or political confines. Some of us want to burst those boundaries in a public way through protesting, writing books, or supporting certain organizations. Others prefer to do it privately through reflection, retreats, meditation, and small personal changes. We keep getting up, and sometimes falling down, because we are drawn to a higher consciousness, to a wiser, more loving, more creative experience of existence.

Whenever I sense that my answers to life's questions are inadequate, I go on an exploration. It's when the worldview I find myself holding feels too small, too confining that a new search begins. Pushing the boundaries of my own knowledge and experience eventually causes a Pop! And it feels like a bubble has burst. Now I can see more broadly, accept more compassionately the foibles of my fellow humans as well as my own, and have a deeper appreciation for the complexity of what we call our world.

I've finally come to realize that there is no end to new vistas, just a limitation of how much energy I have left before my time here is up. As Jane Roberts, author of *Seth Speaks: The Eternal Validity of the Soul* and many other channeled books, put it:

Yet ultimately it seems that the answers to the most important questions only lead to more meaningful questions in which terms like "yes" or "no," "true" or "false," "real" or "unreal" finally vanish in a greater context of experience large enough to contain the incongruities, eccentricities and seeming contradictions in which our greater reality happens.

The key word in that quote is "experience." This book does not, and will not, ask you to take anything on faith. It is meant to open a door to your own inquiry, giving you some insights from explorers who have taken this journey, from within our space/time dimension and beyond it.

Philosopher Joseph Felser speaks to our longing for more direct experience and less dogma in his book, *The Way Back to Paradise*:

For many years, in many quarters, there's been a longing for, an eager anticipation of, a new world religion that would somehow overcome the defects and shortcomings of all the old myths and solve all our problems for us, once and for all. What I have tried to show in this book, is that the new religion — the new worldview — will be each individual's open-ended inquiry into their own experience of the great mystery, in gratitude and wonder, with no strings attached. When we embrace this quest, we make the future here and now.

The Way of Multiplicity and The Way of the One

The sages say "There are many paths," and the history of the wisdom traditions shows the truth of that. The *concept* of God has been evolving over the millennia. Carl Jung,* in his stellar book *Answer to Job*, makes the point that poor Job in the Old Testament was begging God to offer compassion for his suffering. What Jung brilliantly showed was that the biblical story was an allegory. It spoke to the need for a new model of God — the chosen people had moved on from the mean and spiteful image of their god to a more merciful one. "God" was not keeping up.

"God" is an evolving concept as well as an ineffable reality. Looking for the next formulation of an explanation for our existence as a prior one is wearing out is a continuous adventure. Existentialist philosopher Rollo May called it "looking for the god beyond god." But how to describe the next level of awareness is almost by definition impossible because all of our language is tied to the old formulation and images.

Here's another vantage point from psychologist Lawrence LeShan:

> All major schools of mysticism agree that there are two basic states of consciousness important for man. There is the everyday one, which we might call the way of multiplicity. Here objects and events are seen essentially as separate and individual.... The other state of consciousness is sometimes known as the way of the One. Here everything is considered as part of a great pattern of being, of a dynamic interacting field in which there is no possibility of anything being separate, of standing alone. In the first of these, we are well trained and expert. From childhood we learn to function in the world of multiplicity, in the second of these, we are untrained and hardly function at all.

In these few words, LeShan summarizes two different states of awareness that have been available to human beings for as long as we've possessed consciousness. Countless arguments have arisen over the centuries as to which one is "real" as opposed to imaginary; which one leads to a better, happier life, and whether there's any overlap or integration of the two within an individual lifetime. That last point is what Frances and I hope to provide for you: a glimpse of the nature of reality that doesn't deny the validity of the material space/time dimension that we live in during an incarnation *or* the greater reality that we also live in while we're incarnate. Better yet, Frances and I will demonstrate how to find a balance or integration of the two within a lifetime on earth.

Others have wrestled with the paradox of Multiplicity/One...

> *We live in succession, in division, in parts, in particles. Meantime within man is the soul of the whole; the wise silence, the universal beauty, to which every part and particle is equally related; the eternal ONE.*

— RALPH WALDO EMERSON, FROM HIS ESSAY
THE OVER-SOUL (1841)

Outside Sources

In our exploration of "the greater reality" we hear words from the field of parapsychology such as *telepathy, near-death experiences* (NDEs), and *communication with the other side*. From the world of the mystics we hear *Unity Consciousness, Ground-of-All-Being, Allah, God, the One*. From the world of advanced science the term *non-local consciousness* is now often heard. You may have negative feelings about some of these words, but please try to leave all such baggage at the door. One of the most consistent words that comes from explorers is "ineffable" — unable to be described in words.

The explorer has the prerogative to use the words that best fit her or his way of holding the experience. More challenging yet may be ideas presented that seem foreign or completely counter to the way you see things now. Try to hang in there.

Within this book there are also references to other channeled works, to tarot readings (which I do for myself on a regular basis), and to authors whom you may not know. I've tried to elucidate unfamiliar references in the **Endnotes**. I chose not to remove such references from Frances's comments so that we would not lose important insights. Please try to ride with the unfamiliar. This book is an anchor during a chaotic time filled with confusion and suffering. It offers a larger frame, a wider lens, a broader bandwidth, a greater reality.

One word that pops up again and again is "consciousness." It's one of those terms, like "soul" or "nature," that most of us think we already understand. But trying to define it for someone else, or finding any two people who agree on its meaning, is not easy. For our purposes, we'll use this definition: *Consciousness begins with self-awareness and awareness of one's surroundings.* This is known as the "normal state of consciousness." It helps us to negotiate the demands of our physical environment, our emotional and psychological experiences, and interpersonal relations, as well as offering us a sense of past events and possible future occurrences. The effort to *"expand one's consciousness"* generally means to become aware of realities beyond "the normal state."

*(For unfamiliar terms, please see the **Glossary** at the end of the book.)*

Along the Way

Many other fine channeled or automatic-writing books have been published recently, and Frances and I both felt that supporting quotes from a few of those would help the reader understand a particular topic from different perspectives. We have included several excerpts from a book by psychologist Matthew McKay titled *Seeking Jordan* that was sourced through automatic writing. McKay's son Jordan was murdered in San Francisco at age 23, and his despondent father was able to find a way to reconnect with him. Another kindred spirit book, *Testimony of Light*, was channeled to an English nun, Helen Greaves, by her sister nun, Frances Banks, who had departed to a greater reality. Published in 1969, the book contains many descriptions of the "other side" similar to those found in *Seven Questions*.

We also include excerpts from *A Course in Miracles*, from various books by Jane Roberts, and from Francisco Xavier, a Brazilian medium who channeled 400 books over seven decades. He is greatly honored and highly regarded in his native country.

Listening from the Heart

Please remember that this is a journey of inquiry into the unknown, and so it will contain stretches of uncertainty or doubt for you. How could it be otherwise when it is beyond what our conscious awareness tells us is real? Try to let go of the intellectual sparring that will crop up in your mind. Try to listen from the heart, whether or not you agree with or believe any of this. If this book raises questions for you, or brings you more Light, it will have served its purpose.

If you have unresolved issues about a traditional path such as Judaism or Christianity, or unexamined attitudes about religion in general, we suggest reading *The Wave and The Drop* first. It's best to move forward on your spiritual path without carrying the baggage of antipathy toward the classic wisdom traditions. *Wave* is a sincere attempt to find an essential wisdom in each tradition while hinting that it's time to find "the god beyond god." *Wave* does not ask you to accept or forget the faults of the religions that we humans have constructed. But it does suggest that you might want to add further inquiry to your accepted path, or move "beyond" it.

A true explorer recognizes and respects the fact that other explorers describe their experiences in terms and images that make sense to them. This was the case in my dialogues with Frances. She used terms, such as *God*, that I personally felt had too much cultural baggage for me to use in my own inquiries. She also was a student — and then became a teacher — of *A Course in Miracles*, an immensely popular book channeled by Helen Schucman in the 1970s. When we began this collaboration, Frances encouraged me to read it. I tried to, but again, its language style didn't fit my own perspective. That did not at all negate the importance of the material or Frances's love for it. I chose sources for myself, and for my parts of this book, that felt comfortable for me. Frances occasionally commented on current events in our world. She used them as opportunities to share insights from her vantage point. I found some of them startling in that they vastly expanded the scope of my way of looking at those events.

The important message here is that some terms or perspectives offered in this book might create dissonance for you. Remember, these are not "the truth"; these are ways people have expressed what is true for them. All information channeled from the greater reality that has been recorded through the centuries bears the stamp of the personality of the sender and that of the receiver. To listen from the heart is the *sine qua non* of loving communication. We can consider it part of our spiritual practice. The more we can proceed with an open heart and open mind into the next phase of our collective spiritual journey — to evolve with the divine within us — the more joyful, the more magnificent our homecoming will be when we make the transition to the greater reality that awaits us all.

The Seven Questions

As I indicated earlier, the collaboration sessions in this book are not presented in the chronological order in which they were received. They are "clustered" around themes that became the questions. As each of the **Seven Questions** is introduced, you'll find one explorer's answer at the beginning. We encourage you to find your own way to answer it. If a question in the list below intrigues you, go to it first. Your intuition may be telling you it's your best entry point. Each chapter contains a suggested exercise that can bring you an "aha!" moment of insight into the question. Here are the questions we pose for your inquiry:

1. **Am I more than my physical body?**

2. **What's it like "on the other side"?**

3. **What presence fills the universe? God? Oneness? Love?**

4. **How can I *know* there is a greater reality?**

5. **Why does someone incarnate?**

6. **How does one live with the knowledge that there is life after life?**

7. **Where is Home?**

Text Notes: *"C:"* indicates that ***Cynthia*** is the speaker. *"F:"* indicates ***Frances*** is the speaker. Words in brackets [ ] were added by C for greater clarity; F's words are verbatim except for very minor editing; *[smile]* came through as a feeling tone.

Words or phrases marked by * indicate that a further explanation can be found in the ***Glossary*** or ***Endnotes***.

Am I more than my physical body?

Finding a Larger Frame

❧

Who we think we are dies,
but we are not who we think we are.

— Anonymous

What happens to our bodies when we die? They rejoin the elements of the earth in one form or another. Is that the end? Does anything survive? Individual existence after death has been the province of religions and some philosophies, and if it's held as true, it's assumed that happens in some very far-off place. A place that no one can visit beforehand.

Now however, *there is a growing awareness that there is life after life, and it can be visited, albeit very briefly.* That awareness comes from reports of survivors of near-death experiences (NDEs) as well as people describing out-of-body experiences (OBEs). Many describe going to beautiful and strange worlds unlike anything on earth — much more light- and love-filled than anything they've ever known.

In recent decades, tens of thousands of stories of NDEs have been recorded, archived, and studied. These accounts include testimonies from people who were expected to die within a day or so, and from those who were pronounced "clinically dead" who describe visiting another realm that felt very real to them. Likewise, other people have experienced their consciousness as somehow existing outside of their body, either in familiar space/time, or beyond in other dimensions. They describe travels to realms where loved ones, formerly incarnate, now reside. Another source of this kind of awareness is from accounts of channeling (such as automatic writing) that you, dear reader, are now about to experience. Let's begin.

∽◎

C: Good evening, Frances.

F: Good evening!

C: How would you answer the question: Am I more than my physical body?

F: I'd begin by pointing out that something beyond the physical enlivens the body. A body without that "something" is called dead. So many names have been given to it. I'll use *soul* and consciousness. By whatever name, it is the eternal, inviolate part of our being that survives death and moves into the greater reality. It's the simple sense of aliveness we have in our earth lifetimes when we perceive the greater expansion of Love, Joy, Beauty, Harmony. What is that if not something more than the physical body?

We are beings of Light primarily, not dense matter. What we do as earthlings has a profound effect on who we are as beings, but the body and mind are not the only parts of us that are active during our "lifetime." We are conscious beings whose consciousness extends into many dimensions. What we do and say on earth is often influenced by those "higher-being" parts of ourselves.

We have a right, an obligation really, to express as much of ourselves as we can while incarnate. No one knows the true extent of his or her being.

C: What can we do to become more aware of our "higher" selves?

F: Walk a lot. Pray. Expand your arena of activities to include life's pleasures and joys as well as your service and responsibilities. Messages come through the joys, the ecstasy as much as through things like meditation, yoga, chanting.

C: What does a "fully alive" person look like?

F: Like you, like me when I was alive. No different. Just happier than most, content to take life as it comes and ride the waves of joy and sorrow, grief and melancholy.

C: What piece of wisdom can you share today?

F: God is great. The God I know encompasses all there is that I can perceive and imagine. It is so spacious here where I am, still murky, not as brightly lit as I can tell it will be. I must be patient as I sort through all the memories, deeds, missteps, etc. of my former life. It takes a while, but it's all a process that anyone who dies must go through. It's not pleasant, but necessary.

C: Can you "see" what's going on here on earth?

F: I can, and choose not to focus on it. But [I do see that] it's important for you and others to hold onto the values you have grown in yourselves. To let them ripen as much as possible before you die. You don't have to be an "activist." I know you're worried about that. Stay active in your heart, in your mind, and especially in your soul.

Death as Transition

C: What is the most basic shift in awareness that you want to communicate?

F: Death is a transition to a greater reality. Just getting that one across will be a gamebreaker in terms of how people will relate to their lives here. How much more jubilant will those people be who will hear the message from someone as trustworthy as you. They *know* it already. They just need permission — a liberation from the shackles of materialism — to join the ranks of those who rejoice that they are alive and know they will be more alive after the body falls away. You will too!

I'm looking at ways to strengthen the fabric of the material world, to fulfill earth's purpose (she has one, you know [smile]) to help her children withstand the onslaught.

C: What is the "onslaught" you're referring to?

F: You have inklings of it — the signs are floating around — economic collapse, climate change pressures, war, famine, and the challenges that have always come when the Death/Rebirth card [in tarot*] turns up. What happens may not be what the predictors are saying. There will be more of a systemic collapse than an earthquake or tsunami-type catastrophe. But a sorrowful time for all. Needless to say, but I will, much suffering happens during these shifts because of those who want things to stay the same.

Hats off to all the souls on this side (where I am) who are willing to share what we're learning, what we can see "from the balcony," to help those we've left behind on earth. Parents on this side will be helping their children. The wise elders of all nations who have passed on will gather in the clouds to guide us all in appropriate actions and transitions to greater consciousness.

Whatever you [all] are doing needs to be in alignment with the larger forces moving toward the destruction/creation at this time. You need to be "on the right side of history," so to speak. We are all One and all bonded in Love and interlaced with all species and their intelligence on earth. It is "all connected." Seeing the larger picture will help orient you and guide you toward useful and appropriate actions, rather than panic or confusion or paralysis.

C: Will it be clear to those individuals as to what to do?

F: Yes, and moreover they will be directed by guides and those of us on this side to see and act consistent with moving in a wholesome and holistic [thinking for the whole] direction. Another group offers themselves as martyrs to be of service. They make things "writ large," to show how dysfunctional the current situation is. They also engender the emotion needed to force us to look at the dysfunction. Brave souls who deserve our admiration and gratitude as well as compassion.

People will "take bullets" for others as Aaron Feis did, brave man [Parkland, Florida, school shooting, Feb. 2018]. People will be "first responders" of all kinds. First responders have been trained in what to do. That's what's happening to you — you're in training, although you don't have a lucid sense of it yet. But, trust me, you are in training. We will need many of you to deal with the crush of souls transiting the bridge. "Living" people [will help] on the physical side. "The other side" is not some magical place where everything is immediately "heavenly." [At first] it may be gross, sad, and terrifying to many.

C: Why is death not so scary for me? Am I blocking something?

F: No. You will have a relatively easy death, as compared to others. But don't underestimate the trauma of the passage. Very few have "an easy death."

C: How does each of us contain the pain of witnessing or experiencing all this suffering?

F: Look deeply into suffering situations. Find God in there. I know it is not easy. God *is* everywhere. Jesus saw people suffering, individuals in pain or leading miserable lives and he said, "I know your pain. I share your pain." In some cases, he alleviated it because he could. We could too if we recognized we have Jesus's power to do that. Gifted healers do. They know how to "reach in" and soothe the hurt on an ethereal level. Pain is a message, a signal that something needs help — a surrender to a larger agenda for our soul.

C: What about someone who loses everything in a fire, or a flood? Life turns from ordinary to a tragedy of huge proportions overnight.

F: You say, "I'm so sorry. I feel your pain." You have no idea why this house burned down and the one next door didn't. We accept the existence of suffering by becoming mortal. Taking physical form is so complex, so many levels and connections with others. Easier to see from where I am.

Even the most grotesque suffering, seeming so unjust, has a purpose. Impossible to see when you're incarnate. Impossible to understand while you're experiencing it. Just know that there are no accidents. Even something like the randomness of the Las Vegas shootings [59 people dead in 10 minutes in October 2017] — I know you've been pondering this one — has a purpose. What that is, we can't know. Not even me in this state. Maybe I will, maybe you will, at some point in our conscious development.

The Union Continues

C: Many people, including me, wonder if we'll be reunited with those we love after we die.

F: The bonding between and among people, and with their animal partners, continues "on the other side." Knowing that will help diminish the terrible grief people feel, as in the Florida [school shooting] tragedy. That's not to say that it's a loss that should be glossed over. By no means. It hurts terribly to lose someone you love. But after the physical loss becomes more normalized, there is always the spiritual being-to-being connection that endures. Many couples separated by physical death reunite swiftly on the other side — one waiting for the other. These bonds are deep and form a microcosm of the immense bonding of the Whole.

[And another principle is] Service here on earth, while here, and then continued after death. See whatever you're doing as service — high or low.

C: Shall these principles form the basis of a new book?

F: Yes! Time is short before books won't make a difference. If we apply ourselves to this task, we will galvanize others, and the message will ripple out. But time is short. That's why I'm glad you chose to do this tonight. Let's meet as often as possible. We together can make a contribution to the shift in consciousness going on across the planet, within the minds of so many people.

You are right in thinking this is a shift, "an evolution of the God concept" as you like to call it. God isn't shifting, but our ability to access what it is that prompts our God ideas is growing exponentially. It's required due to changing conditions on earth certainly — population growth, climate change, autocrats emerging to take advantage of things falling apart as they must.

What I'm hoping we can do, along with many others, is stop the moral decay setting in. There is a more enlightened consciousness — more people seeing the value of harmony, collaboration, ecosystemic balance. But the sheer size of the whole human enterprise is causing the structures to wobble, to lose their integrity.

[Note from Cynthia: This book is meant not only to provide a spiritual primer on crossing over the threshold into a greater reality, but also to offer insights, because those upheavals Frances mentions are going to cause many more deaths than in normal times. So at one point I asked:]

C: Are we writing an epitaph for our species?

F: No. Not for the species, but for many who will perish in the upcoming upheavals. We want to make the transition easier for them, plus leave behind some new/old ways of holding mortality, life on earth, being more than the physical form.

C: What can we say that will lessen the pain?

F: The principles we arrived at last night plus a few more. We must craft them so they enter the hearts of our readers, bypass their minds if necessary [if resistant].

C: So the principles so far are:

1. There is no death, only transition to an alive greater reality.

2. Bonds of love are so important to the individuals and to the Whole. And they last beyond a lifetime, until "bond" is no longer the operative word. All becomes One.

3. The role of service, making life's purpose service to each other and to the Whole. There are so many ways to do that, as many as there are people. But a task for earth incarnation is to choose one or a few, if possible. Whatever you choose, as long as it has

the strong character of service, will serve you and
be a gain for all.

F: In the end [death], the only thing that matters is "Did
I serve well?" Not what the service was, or how great or
small. It's the value of the service that contributes, not
the content.

C: I think we need some ground rules for the present and
near future that are focused on individual and small collective action, at least for the folks who may pay attention to
this book. We've heard plenty of big-picture, abstract exhor-
tations to shift our mindset. How do we speak to those who
will in fact bear the brunt of the chaos because of lack of
resources or age or isolation?

F: Each and every being is inviolate — once formed there is
no destruction, just absorption into a larger and larger sense
of Unity. Maybe far beyond where I can see now, there is the
moment when the drop is entirely lost within the wave. But
most beings are not close to that yet.

Life After Life

C: How are you doing?

F: I'm fine *[laughs]*. Too trite. I'm going through a process of
cleansing my "outer garments," so to speak. I'm taking a good
look at each lifetime I've lived — am living — and deciding
which ones to carry on, which ones to let go into another
dimension.

C: Sounds like a wardrobe closet.

F: It is in a sense. We [each] put on a persona, one for each lifetime. Some of us have enormous closets full. But we love each one for its courage, and perseverance, and mistakes that helped all of us in our soul group learn from.

C: Do you know what you'd like to learn next?

F: No. My spirit guides are right here with me, and I trust their judgment on what's best for me in the next phase. Many choices. We still have freedom of choice here. There's not a curriculum we have to follow. I'm interested in knowing more about Life in a larger sense, not just the earth life I shared with you and others.

～❦

"So this is death!" I recall saying to one of the Sisters (spirit escorts) who was beside me — "Life separated by density — that's all!" Elation filled me. I knew now that I could "tune in" and even "see" the earthplane, if desire was strong enough to loosen the barrier between your world and my new one... I did not feel that I had really gone away into a far country...I could still keep in touch... . How I longed to materialize before you to show there is no death; but that was beyond my power to do.

— FROM *TESTIMONY OF LIGHT*
(FRANCES BANKS SPEAKING FROM THE OTHER SIDE
TO HELEN GREAVES)

....

EXERCISE

To help you discover where you are on the question of life after life, consider this: If someone you loved were dying and asked you: "Do you believe in an afterlife?" what would you say? Use the space below to jot down some thoughts.

....

What's it like "on the other side"?

A Greater Reality

If you identify with your body alone, then you may feel that life after death is impossible... . Think of yourself as a physical creature now. Know that later you will still operate through another form, but that the body and the material world are your present modes of expression.

— JANE ROBERTS/SETH

Reports of visits to "a greater reality" from the perspective of those alive on earth have created an avalanche of interest, as measured by the number of books, research papers, and conferences now available all over the world. What about reports "from the other side?" Contemporary interest was sparked in the 1970s with the publication of *Seth Speaks: The Eternal Validity of the Soul,* a book channeled by Jane Roberts, followed by a dozen more books she produced with Seth as well as with other discarnate entities, including philosopher William James. [He died in 1910.] Jane's channeling sessions were all recorded, mostly by her husband taking notes, but also some in audio and a few in video. The whole Jane Roberts collection is archived at the Yale University Library.

Other channeled books appeared, including *A Course in Miracles* (1976), which has sold several million copies and is still used as a source by many individuals and study groups today. The channeled books that have stood the test of time each describe life after life from the perspective of an entity "on the other side." No two are exactly alike because they reflect the personality of the entity as well as that of the channeler. However, certain consistent patterns are discernible. Quotes in this book from other channeled materials represent perceptions shared by many of our chosen sources.

~⊛

C: How are you doing?

F: I'm experiencing wonderful new things that can't be described except to say they are marvelously expansive, showing me how limited my perceptions were while "alive." This "place" is a lot like what I imagined heaven to be, only more fun. I can rest, be challenged, be in many places at once. It's unbelievable. Saints have described it, but no one took them seriously. At least I didn't. This underscores the Tao — what can be described is not the Tao. You must experience it.

Earth is an experience too. Quite amazing when you see it "in a larger frame." The difference is that from here, I know there's so much more I can't perceive. Not so on earth. We wear blinders most of the time. [emphasis on "most of the time"]

We're caught up in limitations of time sense and place sense. Wait till you get here! There are no limits, just what your own capacity and evolution allows you to know, experience, love, and explore.

C: Say more about "expansive."

F: I am involved in many things as I was on earth. You have so many choices here to be and do what you want. It all has a feeling of expansion. "Growth" doesn't quite fit because it implies an end point, at least on earth. Expansion of self includes so much more awareness of connection to others, to our own other lifetimes which I can participate in now and help shape into better outcomes. It's all so fluid, free and malleable in the sense that God allows us to become in so many directions. For a "younger soul," it's dizzying, and that's where mentors come in to show the paths and ways of being that will produce the greatest understanding, the most inclusive heart space. That's the driving force — God's love. You cannot get enough of it to say "I'm complete," or "I'm done." Its allurement is omnipresent. Yet there's no pressure, no overwrought desire as in sex or food gluttony. There's a delicious sense of fulfillment in every moment, yet a sense of vibration that wants to reach higher frequencies, other melodies. Each soul provides a unique melody that blends into a magnificent orchestration of music — the Music of the Spheres. No one is "out of tune." Even the less adept have a knowing of how to fit in.

There's also unlimited joy here that is tempting to just luxuriate in, all so life-affirming in a much larger sense than we mean it when we are incarnate. The universe is alive with the sounds of music, to use a popular earth-based saying. I'm beginning to get a better grasp of how things work around here and enjoying the freedom to explore whatever I want.

[Note from Cynthia: I had read a section of the Helen Greaves book, Testimony of Light, *and came across a similar sentiment from her channeling source. The entity that was Frances Banks spoke about Festivals of Light that she attended in the greater reality:]*

> *"There is a swelling of harmony until a particular chord or note is reached and held. That note seems to be the key, the aim, the object of the ceremony...the Note, when at last reached and sounded in full, is held and vibrated at a pitch of intensity which sweeps every soul into harmony. Then Light breaks through into the assembly. Light surrounds us, lifts us, touches us, awakens us."*

C: Can you say more about the transition from this life to the next, the one you're living now?

F: I found the transition difficult, as most people do. Letting go of the security and familiarity of the body's density is a challenge. But once I got clear of the earth plane, I was able to relax into the living embrace of many relatives and friends on the other side.

It's something like coming out of a darkened movie theater into bright sunlight. It takes some adjustment. But the Light of this world of earth-like, but more real, aspects of nature and dwellings is beyond description. Let me just say that the experience of this side, when one fully accepts that one is dead on earth while alive in this greater reality, fills me with a joy beyond comprehension. Like so many people who've experienced NDEs and lived to talk about or write about it, it's a taste of what awaits.

I think the important point for us to convey right now is that the reality of life in another dimension is what awaits all of us. If you can accept that as a guiding principle, then you will live your life according to higher values. It's about expanding the Light of Consciousness, and within that expansion is a Love beyond compare and communion with beings you have loved on earth and many you didn't know you loved because they were or are involved in other lifetimes with you.

C: Frances Banks says it's not easy to connect with the earth plane. Is that your experience?

F: Most souls when they arrive here want very much to connect back to earth loved ones. Most of those on earth only have a vague sense of connection. They usually hold it as "wishful thinking" or as a way to get past the loss. The incarnate ones have very little idea of how much we would like to communicate with them. Also the channels who can really deliver on clear messages from those of us here are few and far between.

There are many more people, like two of your friends, who are each sensing the need for mediums between the worlds. They will practice and get better at it. It's like having a bank of telephones to reach Earth, with long lines wanting to get their chance. I am so glad you are open to this form of communication.

C: What is it like for you now "on the other side"?

F: Lovely. Restful. Busy in the sense of so much to see and learn.

C: Can you tell me something you've learned there that you didn't know here?

F: Much of what we as "alive" [incarnate] beings take for "real" is only partially so. There are shared illusions which then take on a quality of the real.

C: Such as?

F: Climate change. It's risen as this bogeyman, and it is threatening, but it's only the natural expression of how we humans have discovered and used fossil fuels. A very bright person — I'm sure there are some — could have predicted the crisis the world is in now, based on extrapolation. It's all right. It's natural and a predictable development in view of many humans' intense drive for pleasure, convenience, plus greed and illusions of power. All natural and predictable.

Intuition Opens the Door

C: What do you know about intuition that you didn't know when you wrote the book *Awakening Intuition*?

F: Nothing prepared me for what's happening now. I can see so much more, know so much more than I did alive. I'm going to try to put into words what I understand now, and we may have to return to this to smooth it out and have it make sense.

Intuition is a gift from God from "the other side," from the deepest parts of our psyche that we can tap and that's connected to the larger whole. It's a banquet; it's a Ferris wheel.

[C has an image of a Ferris wheel with little hanging chairs, offering goodies]

There's so much to choose from that we have to narrow down into our small space/time place. But it's always there for the asking, for the taking. It's God's way of speaking to the divine within us. God to Self. Self to God, a communication of the highest order.

Whatever we'd like to know within the frame of our consciousness, we can know, can access, can bring into being.

What can I say that will convince people that intuition is nothing special? It's not just for "gifted people." That's a kind of hoarding the riches for the elite that we're all familiar with in other realms — wealth, information, spiritual insight, etc.

Tap it by asking, by expecting, by demanding that you have access to the highest consciousness you have reached at your best moments. Now, every day, in every endeavor — expect, ask, demand that you see all the implications, all the possibilities.

[pause]

What goes around comes around. Putting out the request comes back 10-fold, 100-fold. You have no idea what's available until you put yourself in the way of grace — that grace being wisdom from a higher place, from whatever you want to name your source — God, Allah, an acorn, Jesus Christ, the all-knowing Cosmos — it cannot be named correctly. But it can be experienced.

C: How can we best use intuition?

F: Totally. We can live in an intuitive place, interacting with others who are just using intellect or emotion or rote learning to govern their lives. We can imbue our life with an aura of creativity, harmony, beauty to each and every thing we do.

For example, take a dog who is wandering around, sniffing things. [It] looks pretty mundane. It's picking up clues, putting together a larger picture of who's been here, how long ago. Did anything interesting happen? They are using their intuition all the time, not hamstrung by do's and don'ts and set ways of thinking. Be like that dog — taking in information, allowing it to process, and making decisions based on that much larger field of possibilities. Intuition helps to narrow down the choices to: "I think I'll go in that direction."

Say it's a tracking dog. How much does it have to depend on its intuition? A lot. Tracking is not a simple skill set. It involves "a sixth sense." What we call it in humans — intuition. But it's just the same for all creatures — large and small. I imagine most creatures on earth use it all the time. We humans probably tapped into it for survival in the earliest days of our species. How cumbersome our large analytic brain has become.

C: How else can intuition help?

F: Intuition cuts through verbiage like the earthly chain saw. A mass of tangled branches from a fallen tree. Need a chain saw to clear away and open the path again. [Otherwise] what we see is not what we get. We see what we want to see. We get what our conglomerate of needs, desires, dreams, hopes, fears, loves draw into our lives. We see a person who we can be friends with, maybe love. All outward appearances check out. That person brings along a huge stew of past lives, current preoccupations, and much else to the table, or relationship.

C: What else do you know now that you didn't know, or weren't conscious of, while incarnate?

F: Great balls of Fire. The universe has these magnificent stars/suns that we only see vague pictures of. You could spend much "time" just thrilling to the spectacular light show that God puts on all the time, in so many colors beyond our comprehension. Even mine at this vantage point.

What I've learned to some extent is how much more dimensional — for lack of a better term — Reality is than we can imagine at our best. So many beings, so many colors. So many dimensions — although that term can trip us up because we keep using Space/Time as our touchstone.

Life on the Other Side

C: How are you today?

F: Well. Dancing with the stars, so to speak. What a delightful universe I've picked to land in/spend "time" in. They're all different, you know. We each construct our own.

C: Why are descriptions of the other side so earth-like?

F: We bring over [to this side] what we know. We know our cities and towns and villages. Those are constructs or an architecture in our minds, so to speak. We actually create those structures while incarnate too — I mean, as consensus reality. But that's another topic.

People who come from more primitive backgrounds, like an Amazon village, recreate those scenes here too. It's what you bring with you. Eventually you realize you don't need those structures — that clinging to earth forms — to manage to be here. You can go on to create much more spectacular forms, or not. You can choose to be a ball of light, a form of mainly energy frequencies, but not need a structure to live in. As on earth, those structures, however nice they are, get tedious or burdensome. But the transition from earth to here is handled so beautifully, so lovingly.

C: How do the different "constructs" interact so that it seems like you're sharing one with others?

F: We're all here as energy beings. We interact on an energy level — too difficult to describe, but "Light" comes close. Imagine different colored rays of Light intersecting. Where they intersect, they create another energy form. Eventually, our consciousness grows to the point where earthlike forms are unnecessary.

C: Why would anyone reincarnate when you can simply hang out in such joy?

F: You're forgetting that all incarnations are concurrent, simultaneous.* Many parts of those souls are not part of an incarnation. Those "parts" are enjoying home and are filled with the Love of God. It's good to be so.

C: Can you give me one description of what it's like where you are?

F: Certainly. Open space, open with trees and flowers nearby. There's not a person on earth whose soul isn't nourished by a good description of such a place. With so many humans on the planet, open space becomes a metaphor for the vastly more spacious worlds we come from, and return to, around our incarnations, lifetimes on earth.

We long for those spaces. I love listening to the angels sing, where I am now. I'm surrounded by beautiful colors, sounds, feelings of God's presence. I can "tune in" to the sounds or choose to focus on my own interior music. It's always available; but as on earth, I have work to do, learnings I have to absorb in order for my soul to evolve toward the One.

But there's no fatigue, no sense of "something will be amiss if I don't attend right now." It's more a drawing toward, a wanting to be in an even greater reality of energy and knowing, and most of all, Love that permeates and deepens with every experience I have here. You just want more, not in a greedy way, but in a way that expands your capacity to be of service, to understand the larger dimensions of the path of the One.

We have so many beings around us to help orient us, to guide our choices, and most importantly, to love us unconditionally. If we can persuade our dear reader that he or she will be loved so deeply and completely when they arrive here, we will make this a very attractive place to want to return to.

Being here is such a joy. There's no [feeling of] "I wish I was more advanced," or "I'm lesser than." All beings that I have the ability to interact with are energy nodes, with their own beauties. There's no competition of any sort, because there's no shortage of anything you need or want. All is Light/Love/Communion. Plenty for everyone. We each sense the calling of the Divine One to emerge. But we can enjoy the ride, so to speak, from whatever vantage point we choose, and by using whatever vehicles we care to. The tortoise makes the journey as well as the hare. I can try either one anytime.

C: What are you studying or learning during your experience of life between incarnations?

F: Love. It's really all about Love. The rest are details. Yes, I'm learning new knowledge because that's what I enjoy. But it's all in the service of deepening my capacity for loving myself and others, and God, of course, which is the Whole experience.

....

EXERCISE

Make a list of everyone (including nonhumans) to whom you can say: "I love you." Make a second list of people and others who you think, or know, love you. If your cultural background or personal comfort does not include exchanging "I love you" with other people, who are the people that you do feel love for, and love from?

....

Attending Your Memorial

C: Can you go back to your memorial and give me some details I wouldn't know about?

F: Yes. It was marvelous, wasn't it? I felt so honored. A lifetime achievement award.

I sensed from my children that they were happy for me. Obviously, they were sad at the loss of our earthly connection. But each of them has a sense of this "greater reality" and knew I was "in a better place," not just in the traditional way that's said, but in a happy, expanded place of Light and Love. They knew how much I loved my parents and wanted to rejoin them. They also sensed I had played out the hand I was dealt, in my terms. I could have stayed on as a wise elder, but that wasn't an image I held dearly. I was anxious to be "off to my next great adventure," in the immortal words of Willis Harman.* On some level they knew that and let me go. They have the wonderful tribute that Coleen [Elgin]* made to remind them of who I was. Frances Vaughan will live on in this collaboration and others.

C: Another question: Who was there to meet you when you arrived in the greater reality after you passed on and crossed the bridge?

F: My mother, dear woman. How glorious she looked. I barely recognized her from her appearance, but I knew her on a soul level that connected us immediately. I had a dog I loved as a child, a spaniel, and he was there too. Many friends who had passed before me, such as Rollo May and George McMullen.* It was a reunion of sorts, although at first the transition leaves you disoriented, and you must do a life review before you can move on. Now I must decide on when/

if to return to earth. So many choices [life plans] to make the next passage. I must "regroup" and see what serves my soul best.

C: Can you tell me about another lifetime you're participating in?

F: Yes. I'm living in Siberia, as a Russian fur trader, and am learning about living in a difficult environment. I have a loving wife and children who are learning the trade of trapping, killing, and dressing the furs. My awareness from this past lifetime [as Frances Vaughan] is informing the fur trader to be kind, to dispatch the animal with respect, and leave other parts to share with animals in that area.

C: That's a far cry from California author and transpersonal psychologist.

F: You bet. That's the beauty of a soul group with many facets. We can inform each other from what we're learning in the other lifetimes and from the whole Being in ways that an individual lifetime couldn't do easily. It's part of the Communion aspect we are developing. Communion has so many levels to it — community, commons, integration of parts into a higher ordered Whole.

You and I are blending our minds and souls together to produce this book. It's not one or the other of us. Neither could do this on her own. It's another example of Communion.

C: May it be so.

....

EXERCISE:

Take the time to think about these questions: Who is waiting for me on the other side of the veil? Who would I like to see again? Who will I be an escort for in their transition to life after life when I am on the other side?

....

What presence fills the universe? God? Oneness? Love?

What holds the greater reality together?

≈

*Nowhere have I encountered the furnishings of a
conventional heaven, or glimpsed the face of God. On
the other hand, certainly I dwell in a psychological
heaven by earth's standards, for everywhere I sense a
presence, or atmosphere, or atmospheric presence that
is gentle yet powerful, and all-knowing.... At the risk
of understating, this presence seems more like a loving
condition that permeates existence, and from which all
existence springs.*

— JANE ROBERTS CHANNELING WILLIAM JAMES

Not a single report about existence on "the other side" from a discarnate entity mentions running into a God figure — an individual being who seems to be orchestrating everything. Some reports talk of meeting Jesus, Buddha, Mohammed, or another well-known saintly figure who was incarnate at one time. The description of *God*, from a spectrum of sources, collapses the duality of separation by saying: The divine is within me; I am within the divine. It is summarized well in a verse from *A Course in Miracles*:

> *The recognition of God is the recognition of yourself.*
> *God dwells within.*
> *The journey to God is merely the reawakening of the*
> *knowledge of*
> *where you are always, and what you are forever.*

∾⊘

C: What does the word "God" mean to you?

F: God is all-pervasive, all-knowing, all-loving. God is All and God is nothing but Love.

C: You make God sound like some kind of intelligence, and then say "God is nothing but Love."

F: It's one of those ineffable experiences. I'm immersed in God and it feels like Light, Love, and Communion with all that is, into an eternal Whole. Nothing on earth prepared me for this. You can read accounts of saints, meditate until you're blue in the face (I did a lot of meditation), but you barely graze the immensity of what you experience in the greater reality. And I know I'm only at an early stage of my evolution in knowing God and moving toward Unity Consciousness, or the dissolution of all separateness.

C: Would someone who was able to visit the greater reality, as in an NDE or OBE, be able to sense what you describe?

F: Yes, momentarily. As I said, saints have. People who are "out-of-body" like Bob Monroe* certainly did. But such visitors are rare. And it's probably a good thing, since too much of this and they may not want to return to complete their purpose for their incarnation.

C: So do you want the word "God" to describe what you're experiencing?

F: Very much so since I find it fits my use of the word on earth as something expansive and loving and full of beneficence — something like wanting the very best for all beings. Also, I am always in deep gratitude for my life here in this marvelous place, and it helps to have an entity to be grateful to, even though I know I'm part of it, and therefore [am] grateful to myself as well.

C: Why *not* be grateful to ourselves?

F: Of course. It's a higher understanding. Like praying was for me. When I prayed, I knew I was both supplicant and recipient of the prayer as part of the Whole.

C: What else have you learned since you've been "on the other side"?

F: Many wondrous things. There is a symphony on this side — at least groupings of beings who are living beautifully together, in harmony (to use the analogy to music). Communities with their own culture, their own tunes.

God is here, present. You can feel it in every moment, in every being, in every fabrication of what passes for physical structure. Communication is automatic, like the concept of telepathy, but without even the sense of sending and receiving. Just there.

The loves of my lives are here for me to greet, to love again, to penetrate each other, if we care to — no force — to really appreciate the beauty and the depth of the person they were on earth, but whom we often kept at arm's length for various silly reasons, like stereotypes or "propriety." Here we can love and laugh and truly enjoy each other's gifts. I'm playing piano again and loving how I can dive into the soul of the music for depth I never experienced on earth.

C: What other learnings?

F: More about God — still my favorite term. Now the god beyond god — as Rollo May used to say. He's here, by the way, and we chat from time to time.

(It's hard to explain "time to time" — [it's more like] a simultaneous phenomenon with other things I am doing. Chats happen as an occurrence within the whole sphere of activities — not in some linear way.)

God is all-pervasive, all-loving. At the level I'm at [of knowledge], He/She still feels like a presence around me. I long for the day when I will disappear within the All and have no more individuality. I have much more to learn, much more to absorb — because that's closer to how it feels — an absorption of energy, both a finer quality of energy and a higher vibrational frequency. Now I'm in a world of Love — surrounded, permeated, drenched in it, as it were.

I can see the limitations of my last incarnation, which I am holding onto (not put away in the closet yet) in order to stay connected with those I love (including you). I also see how this particular piece of me, of the oversoul in which I participate, could grow more in wisdom and still make contributions, as with this book.

But I'm anxious to "move on" to higher realms, to more advanced mentoring, to join my spirit guides in higher adventures. It's not all harps and roses here. There's a pressure to evolve here — just as much, if not more, than [being incarnate] on earth.

Is God Love?

C: What do you have to share today?

F: I'm going to talk about Love again. It's the biggest topic we can "share" with the living. We know much about it here on the "other side." We see its effects in everything — lots of love here, lack of love there. What we know [on earth] is that to cultivate love in all its aspects, in all its forms, is key to "everlasting life."

C: Do you cultivate love "on the other side"?

F: Yes, indeed! All the time, without hesitation. So many opportunities to find love here, to show love to those struggling, to know love at a deeper level yourself.

C: Is God Love?

F: Yes and No. Yes: He/She is the glue that keeps it all together. No: in that there are other dimensions of reality — other realities, really [smile at pun] that make their "glue" from wisdom, creativity, etc. Of course, love is involved in those activities but [it is] not as prominent.

What I know from here (where I am now) is that Love conquers all. It's true. We can bring Love to the harshest situation, to the most dire person or place, and rejuvenate the soul, the spirit. It's always there. But it can become so worn down, so miserable in its existence (not only on earth, but for those newly arrived here too) that only the touch of Love from someone, sent from somewhere else, can reach it.

We are sending each other signals all the time — right, left, up, down. Signals coming from each person to each person.

C: How can one person receive all those signals?

F: Because we are transmitter/receptor beings with infinite capacity (our bandwidth, in current parlance). We know we are reaching/feeling a greater Whole. It's intoxicating in a way. We calm down to assimilate, and expand again to the tune of the dimension you're in. So many dimensions, so many tunes.

Is Awareness of the Greater Reality Expanding on Earth?

C: Is there a "greater reality" movement or revolution in cosmology happening on earth?

F: Yes and no. *No* in the sense that it's not a "visible movement" as we generally think of it. *Yes* in the sense of ground-breaking, earth-shaking changes in perception. For Pope Francis to say "there is no hell," or more correctly, nothing that constitutes eternal damnation, is revolutionary for the Christian church. The fiction of hell holds people captive not only in their behavior (which is bad enough) but it imprisons them in their thinking, in their minds — which is worse than any physical prison — more deadly to the soul.

Yes, we make terrible mistakes, or act out of very self-centered motives, causing untold suffering. But given a larger framework on the whole of space/time existence, it is a baby learning to walk and falling down, or breaking something expensive, or hurting a sibling.

I know it's hard to understand, and seems to trivialize horrible suffering. But when you reach this stage [where I am] it looks much more forgivable. It's the message of love that's pouring into your dimension from many sources — for example, Pope Francis encourages all of us to embrace diversity. Sharon Salzberg [speaks of lovingkindness] in Buddhism, Jane Roberts and others [speak of group souls] in the afterlife cosmology arena. Your world needs this message so badly because the forces that promote hatred and tribalism and violence are running rampant and will continue to do so.

The messages of love are like an antidote to the poison. We don't know yet whether the poison will kill the species. It's touch-and-go. But we (on this side and yours) are pushing the antidotal medicine in as many ways as we can. As I've pointed out many times, we each need to be reaching out to the audience we can reach through as many avenues as we can.

C: I'm sobered by your suggestion that we're poisoning ourselves in so many ways, and how Love is the antidote. But we don't know if it's going to be enough to save our species.

F: I know that to be true, and I don't know the answer to "Is it enough?" There are those who have greater access to the span of "time" and can see the past and future much more broadly. I am not one of those. I can see more than you because "the blinders" are off. But that doesn't mean I see everything. Just like you wanting to push the boundaries of your consciousness farther and farther out (to use space/time language), I want to also. It's all a process of evolution. That's the term we use, although it still implies a time continuum. Hard to explain.

C: What about the story itself? It's all love, "atmospheric presence" of an indescribable feeling of Love/Light/Communion that pervades the realms my guides are in. I'm beginning to wonder if it's just a "story," the next iteration of the God concept.

F: It is. There's no way to find language for what this is like — the NDE people try, but they fall short of the experience itself. It is a heaven beyond description, beyond concept.

C: What about the dark, evil forces that some people talk about? Where does that live and how do we integrate that into the picture?

F: Dark is the absence of Light — the only way we can describe it to you. Yes, there are areas of No Light, No Love, No Communion. Just abysmal pain and separation. [So my message is:] Stay connected. Deepen your love for everyone, for everything you see, hear, touch. The pain of those teenagers marching today [Parkland, Florida students]* caused that huge outpouring of "We want to stop this pain. Enough!"

How to do it without creating more division, more pain? They are on the road to discovering that Love heals, and that their love for each other, across diverse boundaries, grows them individually, and all of us — and I mean "us here too" — immeasurably. Today was a huge outpouring of Love. It took all the ugly incidents to become a "saturated solution,"* as you like to say, to catalogue this new movement. It won't be perfect. Nothing human ever is — by design.

Whatever you decide to do will be fine in the service of the Whole. You don't have to march, or to feel guilty. Your job now is to figure out this new form of spirituality washing over the planet. It's growing, not only in book count and movie theme, but within the consciousness of the collective.

Hell: True or False?

C: What about hell? I've learned it exists, but only if you create it yourself, individually. No one imposes it on you, and it doesn't last forever.

F: Hell. We often create hells on earth for ourselves by bad choices we make. By finding it easier to hate and cheat and dominate others. Love isn't easy until you really get it that it's the substance of everything and it's unadulterated — [there's] no mixture of love and hate, or love and superiority here. Just love.

C: How does one get rid of those nagging remnants of lesser emotions?

F: They wash out. In our energy forms, beautiful as they are, we are also transparent. We "see" each other's dark spots, unclean corners. There's no hiding or camouflage.

As for hell, there is definitely a lower level of self-imposed pain and terrible suffering [after death] when individuals refuse to see what pain they've caused others, or are stuck in cesspools of hatred.

C: Why wouldn't someone just really work to move out of those areas when they see how ugly they are?

F: Why don't people move out of them while incarnate? Same reasons. Occasionally someone sees "the error of their ways"

— a cult leader or a neo-Nazi says," I've seen the Light and it is Love," and means it. But there's a perverse pleasure, at least on earth, of wallowing in a self-indulgent hatred, or a strong sense of "how superior I am compared to others." Each of us is guilty of at least a small amount of that along the way.

C: I've heard that spirit guides reach out to those in their own hell [after death]. The guides and the loving family members never give up on inviting a tortured soul into the Light and Love and Communion with the One.

F: That's true. And some good souls, still incarnate, even offer to work from their side to move the souls in hell to a better place. You're in no danger of going to hell, although you were told you were as a teenager. Perhaps [that was] a useful fiction to keep some out of trouble. More important is the realization that the One is all-embracing and [that] we want all souls to move into greater and greater experiences of Light. When our species has played itself out on earth, all beings will be on a path toward the One.

Spirit Guides

C: Can you say more about spirit guides?

F: They are everywhere and always available. But they don't always respond in the ways we want them to. They have a higher vantage point and know the "pacing" of a lesson to be learned. So they don't always jump in with answers to our requests.

C: Who are they, and how do we access them?

F: Just ask. Each individual human has several assigned at birth. Sometimes others come along during a lifetime to assist in a special way. They do have individual tasks and skills, as other sources suggest.

So ask. Ask and you shall receive, but not necessarily in the ways you ask or the specific action or manifestation you'd like. The request must come from a deeper knowing that something will be helpful at this point in your journey. Certainly, requests that bring more Love and Light into your world are the kinds you need to focus on.

There are lesser spirits whose focus is to deter you, slow you down, or even seduce you into thoughts and acts that are detrimental to your soul's journey. Be careful what you ask for! There are discarnate spirits who would like you to join them in their misery. Misery loves company! *[smile]*

C: So how can we know if our request to a spirit guide is in our best interest, our higher self?

F: Test it out in your mind. Follow the trajectory created, if the request was granted. This is much more difficult than it might seem. What if you asked for restored health after a terminal diagnosis? What if you asked for safe passage for a loved one going to a dangerous place? Very legitimate requests, it seems. But you don't have access to the full picture of what that diagnosis or a misfortune in a dangerous environment is meant to create for you. [Might be] just the challenge you, or the traveler, was set to have. A spirit guide will not interfere with that kind of plan.

As for "astral low-lifes," as someone once called them, those are potholes in the road. Remember that Jesus and Mohammed and many other saintly people were tempted by spirits bent on knocking them off their purpose. They didn't succeed. But those of us with lesser defenses can be sidetracked. If so, when you recognize it, pick yourself up, forgive yourself, and move on.

The question to ask is: "Does my request or intention that I'm petitioning spirit guides to help on bring more Love, more Light to my life and those around me? Or is it strictly self-serving?" Sometimes it's hard to tell. You can fool yourself. We all do on occasion.

Spirit guides of the highest order we can attract on our journey are there to serve as mentors, guides, provide assistance, and yes, protect us from lesser beings, both while we are incarnate as well as here "on the other side."

C: Do you have spirit guides now?

F: I do, and can garb them in any way I like. So I have one with me now who's tall and winged, just like the medieval paintings. They are beings of Light. They don't wear clothes, but [I clothe them] for the sake of my needing a visible presence at this point in my journey.

C: What do you ask your angel for?

F: More Light. More ways to understand my unique contributions and to put me in the way of grace to accomplish it. I ask for more capacity to love, more people to love and learn from. When it's clearly a positive, affirming request, it can happen instantaneously. I asked for you to be a collaborator with me, and look what happened!

Ask intensely —
like a straight line engraved toward the object you want;
pray with desire —
as though you interrogated your own soul about its
deepest, most hidden longings;
and you will receive expansively —
not only what your desire asked,
but where the elemental breath led you —
love's doorstep, the place where you bear fruit and
become part of the universe's power of generation
and sympathy.

— TRANSLATION OF MATTHEW 7:7 OF NEW TESTAMENT,
AS INTERPRETED IN *DESERT WISDOM* BY NEIL
DOUGLAS-KLOTZ

....

EXERCISE

Do you have conversations with a personal divinity? Do you trust that you are protected by a spirit guide or angel? Do you ask a parking fairy to help with a parking space (many people do)? What's your sense of the reality of these exchanges?

....

How can I *know* there is a greater reality?

Portals

Intuition allows one to draw on that vast storehouse of unconscious knowledge that includes not only everything that one has experienced or learned... but also the infinite reservoir of the collective and universal unconscious, in which individual separateness and ego boundaries are transcended.

— Awakening Intuition, by Frances Vaughan
(Published in 1979)

I had a heart attack, and I found myself in a black void, and I knew I had left my physical body behind.... in the distance I could see a grey mist, and I was rushing toward it.... Beyond the mist I could see people, and their forms were just like they are on earth, and I could also see something which one could take to be buildings. The whole thing was permeated with the most gorgeous light, a living, golden yellow glow....

Yet it wasn't my time to go through the mist, because instantly from the other side appeared my Uncle Carl, who had died many years earlier. He blocked my path, saying, "Go back. Your work on earth has not been completed. Go back now." I didn't want to go back, but I had no choice, and immediately I was back in my body.

※

After several months of intermittent bodily sensations before going to sleep, radio business executive Bob Monroe had his first full-fledged out-of-body experience. He found himself looking down from his bedroom ceiling upon his sleeping body lying next to his wife on their bed. After tests ruling out a brain tumor, or hallucinations, he found he could make the experience happen at will. Monroe discovered he could travel with his "second body," as he called it, anywhere within the space/time dimension, and then beyond. He wrote Journeys Out of the Body (1971) and then two more books on the same subject. He created an audio laboratory where he replicated brain wave patterns using sounds, matching the patterns of other people having OBEs. By listening to those sounds through headphones, many more people *have had similar experiences. The Monroe Institute in Virginia carries on his work.*

≈≈

Mary Neal was a surgeon and kayaker who was declared dead after being pulled from a whitewater rafting accident. Later she recounted being trapped underwater: "I could feel bones breaking. I could feel ligaments and the tissue tearing. I felt my spirit peeling away from my body." She described visiting a domed structure exploding not only with light and color but with love. She talked with spirits who told her it was not her time to die and she returned to life. A few years later, her book about the experience was published: To Heaven and Back: A Doctor's Extraordinary Account of Her Death, Heaven, Angels and Life Again: A True Story *(2012).*

≈≈

These accounts are taken from people who have visited the greater reality. There are thousands of stories from people who have had near-death experiences, out-of-body experiences, mystical experiences. These accounts are found in spiritual tomes, research studies, and stories from "ordinary people" who have the courage to describe an experience that they say convinced them of life after life. Notice that the stories are all based on direct *experience*.

Belief sometimes has to precede experience. Sometimes it follows *from* experience. Some people are thrust into the greater reality by a near-death experience (NDE), or a spontaneous out-of-body experience (OBE). Thousands of people have reported a conscious feeling of being out of their bodies, and the ability to look at their bodies from a distance. Some report the experience as being terribly frightening because they had no belief in such a possibility. But their experience then created the basis for their belief in such events.

Some people approach a portal to the greater reality through curiosity triggered by hearing an amazing remote-viewing* story. Another avenue is being with a loved one in her dying time and hearing her describe the escorts who are waiting to help with the transition, who are "as real as you are." Other people have spontaneous experiences during trauma or dreams, and a door opens.

[Cynthia: When I asked Frances about the best ways to access the greater reality (without a near-death experience), I was taken aback when she started talking about a show she had seen on TV while on earth about making pasta. It turned out to be a great analogy.]

C: What is the basis for accepting this new cosmology — this "greater reality" way of looking at our existence?

F: Quite some time ago, I watched a TV show that featured a man making pasta. He showed the ingredients and then the process. Voila! Pasta. I was struck by how it all came together — his creativity, the ingredients, the "know-how" that resulted in a very beautiful work of "food art." And I imagined it tasted good too. What we're doing is a little like that. We have a goal in mind. In our case, it's to promote the principles, especially the existence, of a "greater reality," as you're now calling it. We have the pieces, the aspects, the guidance to do it well — to make great pasta. But unless we actually gather the ingredients (in our case, words) put them into a bowl [book] in an orderly fashion, work with the recipe to make it the best we can (cooks again!), nothing will happen.

We're about moving people toward a greater sense of consciousness, of love, of the value of their own evolution. That's the goal. Not the pasta itself, but the *experience* of the pasta — the delight, the nourishment, satisfaction. Never lose sight of the fact that this is all about the *experience* of consciousness and how it ripples out to others, to the universe, and ultimately to the One.

When a car is taking you to a destination, whether it's an old Prius (like I had, or you have), or one of those Teslas, you don't think about the mechanics of the car. It's a vehicle, like an incarnation. What you and many others are experiencing is "a new car," a better way of moving along. We've had to leave so many other forms of transportation aside. Who would take a donkey instead of a Tesla? Or just a basic good car? There is a value to the old forms. But for our purposes now, which are to prepare people for major changes in as many ways as we can, the new cosmology is a fine vehicle. Don't forget that it too will be traded in, or reduced back to its elements, after it's completed its mission — getting us along on this next part of our journey.

The Ace of Pentacles you [recently] pulled in your tarot reading is a symbol of a visible, tangible cosmology emerging. See it in the outpouring of books, speakers, movies — writ large, writ small. But visible in its manifestations.

C: Thank you! So helpful. So many different ways of understanding how a form functions to "hold things up," to put the recipe together in the bowl and make the pasta. Without getting hung up on whether the bowl is real, or how pretty or plain it is. What more can you say about the "pasta" we're making?

F: How and why the recipe works. Why does combining all the elements in the pasta program [on TV] result in a fine experience of nourishment? I'm watching myself think about new ingredients, trying "dishes" I wouldn't have considered before — expanding my repertoire, so to speak. We cooks can get jaded in our recipes.

C: I feel like I've added a whole bunch of new ingredients to the "recipe" I am. They haven't quite jelled yet, but I'm sensing a new, more powerful and loving version of myself emerging. *Strength* (a card in my tarot reading today) offers me a glimpse of why this is all worthwhile to me personally. Greater personal strength to carry on in these last years of this lifetime.

F: Very much so. And you have plenty to contribute yet before you leave your dimension. Just not in the ways that you've seen useful before. There's no limit to our contribution. We must mold it within the confines [boundaries] of our life circumstances [that is, inside the bowl]. It wouldn't work if we merely dumped all the pasta ingredients on the tabletop.

So the new cosmology is a container, in a way. A necessary-but-not-sufficient piece of the work to be done. We must make it alive — yeasting new forms of love, community, service, joy, and ways to address greater suffering, which will happen soon.

C: In the book you wrote while incarnate titled *Awakening Intuition*, you talked about the importance of finding our authentic self as a starting point for deeper understanding of what motivates the choices we make on a daily basis — choices that affect our lives for better or worse.

F: Yes. Be true to yourself — find your authentic sense. "Authenticity," for some people, means expressing anger or fear or rage or hurt whenever they feel that particular emotion. The authentic self is much deeper, much wiser in its expression. It knows that emotions cloud thinking, cloud compassion, cloud seeing the other person or situation in its fullness. The lens of the heart always sees God in the other, God's work in a situation.

That doesn't mean that "everything's perfect" in the sense that all tragedies are God's will. It means we take the joyful with the painful and work with what is. The person who died by getting hit by the driverless car the other night has to deal with death. That's what happened. So does the sad family. All terrible to hold. But the person who died has a choice to be angry, get "stuck" in limbo of not wanting to be dead. Or move on to home and oversoul and life between lives to see what was learned in that lifetime. Being more careful crossing the street could be one lesson.

Portals to a Greater Reality

[I asked Frances to suggest ways to access the greater reality open to all of us....]

C: How would you describe, in general, how to access the greater reality, for those of us incarnate?

F: By going in, and by going around. Going into a place of utter quiet, or utter beauty, or utter love. Getting beyond the boundaries of normal reality. And realizing there is so much more to explore, to experience, as you have. Anyone can begin to access the greater reality by simply being open to it. You began decades ago with the tarot. What a useful way to know that there is greater information available, guidance. That the cards fall into meaningful positions when you lay them out. You might even be skeptical at first, but you try it and it starts working for you.

Just try to be receptive to answers, to situations where you could use some help. Instead of *thinking* about the answer in some logical way, give it time to show up. [It] may not be instantaneous, although it can be. It could show up in a book you're reading, or a casual comment by a friend, or in some dream, a symbol like a lemon or a bird that can provide an answer. Try it. It can't hurt.

Once you start trusting that modality of knowing, you'll be turning to it more often. Then you'll begin to wonder where those answers are coming from. That leads to the "curiosity" you mention in the introduction. Then you're in inquiry mode, and it will lead you to broader vistas and ways of knowing.

I was very interested in intuition, and discovered that being open to allowing hunches, feelings to enter and provide insight was as good [as], or better than, "thinking" about it. The first prerequisite is being open to the whole arena of "knowing" beyond your simple senses and the knowledge base you yourself have gathered.

It's out there, or in there, depending on which perspective you prefer. You find out that eventually there is no "out" or "in." It just is. Then you keep on expanding your awareness. Your consciousness grows and reaches out to other entities — your spirit guides. The greater vistas of other worlds are accessible to consciousness when you trust it to reach its potential in your lifetime. Hardly anyone does. I didn't. You won't. But we both have made, and are making, gains in well-purposed lifetimes. And, of course, we bring that gain back to the whole oversoul.

C: What else might we suggest as a good place to begin the inquiry?

F: Psychic [psi] abilities are gateways too. They excite some people. There's so much research on telepathy and remote viewing. Many people are interested in forms of healing that call in greater energies, known as psychic healing. There's precognition — knowing something in advance of its happening. It's scary territory for some. But it's a surefire way of getting you into a fascinating world where there are no explanations for those abilities, only that psi is operating in a mysterious way. And the good news is psi abilities are distributed across the species (other species have it too). It's not some special gift that only a few people have. Most everyone can draw a picture, or play a musical instrument. Some better than others. They have a "talent." But anyone who devotes time and learning to art or music will develop some skill at it. Same with psi. Guaranteed.

C: Where does intuition cross over into psi?

F: Everywhere. Intuition is a growing awareness of energies beyond the physical. If cultivated, it grows beyond good guesses or lucky moments to a real sensing of telepathy, precognition, and so on. Most of us have "intuitions" once in a while. With cultivation, they become psi skills that can be just parlor games or a real service to other people.

C: Anything else?

F: There are tried-and-true ways of deep commitment to spiritual practices such as yoga or meditation. They take time. But each one will get you into a more expansive appreciation of reality beyond the ordinary.

C: What about divination tools such as tarot, astrology, or the *I Ching*?*

F: Those can be useful but [they] necessitate a commitment and rigor to use them as portals to a greater reality. Often they're more like parlor tricks*, where you can fool someone, or yourself, into thinking that the literal symbols are true. You need to develop an awareness that goes beyond the cards or charts or coins that truly delves into another source of insight. Those paths can be gateways, but it's easy to get stuck in the literal interpretations and not develop the psychic-level insights that are the real portals to a greater reality.

Let's not forget other avenues of bypassing the rational and the material. Deep love for God, for humanity, for one other person can open a doorway to greater consciousness. Great beauty, sublime music, poetry — all these can cause that Pop! into an expanded reality. Your soul has to be ready. Those transcendent experiences have been portals for humans for many centuries.

C: More suggestions?

F: Reading a few books can help. [Listed at the back of this book.] But don't get stuck reading books and never trying on your own to *experience* the greater reality. That's the only way you'll ever truly know.

C: I've been working to incorporate more psi abilities into my life, and to accept the existence of "a greater reality." I find sometimes that it makes me feel off balance — which dimension am I living in?

F: Nothing is more important than life on earth for those living it. (This includes you.) You're wrestling with "stepping off the edge," staying centered yet wanting to explore vast dimensions beyond earth's dimension. Well and good. But as you say, pay attention to the ground rules of the dimension you're in. That doesn't just mean don't trip over the curb, or watch out for cars. It means having the sense of being here, not somewhere else, as much as possible. It means having a ride on this planet and enjoying it going round and round, paying attention to its details and learning, learning what you can while you're alive. That's all for now.

In her book Awakening Intuition, *Frances offers this exercise as a good way to begin to develop this way of knowing...*

....

EXERCISE

When you are sitting quietly relaxed, simply hold the word INTUITION in your awareness. You may visualize the word written out before you, or you may repeat the word to yourself as if it were a mantra. If extraneous thoughts and feelings intrude, simply bring your attention back gently to the word INTUITION. Associations and unexpected insights may appear spontaneously and you may wish to record them after the exercise is over. It's usually best to begin with brief periods of concentration (five minutes more or less). The key to amplifying your awareness of intuition is attention.

....

Important reminder: Pay attention to the ground rules of the dimension you're in.

Why does someone incarnate?

Do we have a purpose in being here?

≈©

Physical existence is one way the soul chooses to experience its own actuality. The soul, in other words, has created a world for you to inhabit, to change — a complete sphere of activity in which new developments and indeed new forms of consciousness can emerge.

— JANE ROBERTS/SETH SPEAKS

You and I, dear reader, are *incarnate* — we have a physical body existing in a dimension of dense matter embedded in space/time. Frances is *discarnate* — that part of her that existed on earth until September, 2017, is now gone, but she lives on in a greater reality that she's already described to some extent. Why did each of us, including Frances, you, and me, choose to incarnate?

"Moral gymnasium" is how one explorer of life after life describes the purpose for being on earth. Professor Stafford Betty, who has researched hundreds of channeled accounts, says we are souls in training.

> *"Some athletes prefer to play teams they can beat, but others want stiffer competition. If we are wise, we won't wilt under the pressure of the 'stiffer competition,' the rejection by the one we love, being passed over at work, the tumor — but will fight on.... The Great Spirit has given us a world full of physical and moral challenge, and he hopes that we'll use our freedom to choose the good over the bad, to help out when we can, in spite of tremendous temptation to give up."*

From the other side, our other channeled sources corroborate that view that choosing to reincarnate on earth has an approach/avoidance characteristic (like having to go to the local fitness gym has for me).

- *In* Testimony of Light, *Frances Banks tells us: "I am aware too that in the last life experience I but repeated old struggles. None of it was new. No adventure into matter, into the exterior, is ever entirely fresh or untried. It has all been worked to its end perhaps hundreds of times before, though under different circumstances, perhaps in different worlds.... Now I perceive more clearly, for I am no longer cluttered by illusions, [I see] that the great purpose of life in matter is to illuminate matter with Spirit."*

- *In* Nosso Lar, *the book channeled by Francisco Xavier, the entity Emmanuel says that the essential task of an incarnation is to "acquire an understanding of our infinite potential and that we use it in the service of the good. Earth's human beings have not been disinherited. They are God's children engaged in constructive labor and clothed in flesh, and they are students attending a worthwhile school where they must learn to evolve. The human struggle is their opportunity, their tool and their textbook."*

- *In* Seeking Jordan *by Matthew McKay, his discarnate son Jordan puts it plainly: "The purpose of matter — whether in the form of circling planets or the human body — is to help consciousness grow. All of physical existence serves this purpose. Consciousness creates matter and the laws of the universe. Then it manipulates and lives in physical worlds in order to learn and evolve. So every event is an opportunity for souls to grow."*

The choice to "keep going to the gym" tells us that consciousness is not static. An eternal place in Heaven cannot be gained after one exemplary lifetime. It's clear from our sources that existence demands development of greater and greater understanding, whether in an earth incarnation or somewhere else.

We apparently spend lifetimes on earth learning about and creating a more profound version of reality for ourselves and each other. Lest this makes earth sound too mundane, like a gym or grade school, an incarnation also has its own unique adventures and soul-enhancing peak experiences. Exquisite art, transcendent music, having a baby, or sacrificing one's life to save another are among the infinite choices a life on earth presents. The element common to all of incarnation's best adventures is: Love. The love we create will live on forever — in our hearts while we're on earth, and in our souls when we're "on the other side."

C: Why do we incarnate, come to earth?

F: Earth is not a place for perfect. It's a place of trial-and-error. We all know we incarnate for a purpose. Sometimes that's hidden from our conscious minds.

C: How would you describe what you did?

F: I "fell off the wagon." Not alcoholism, but a narrow-casted version of Christianity that served me in my early days, which I then abandoned. I rediscovered it at a deeper level in *A Course in Miracles* and decided to stick with it. Of course, I listened to wise people on other paths to the One. But I recommend finding a path and holding it gently, to allow for other messages to join in.

Life Review

[*Cynthia: Each and every channeled source I've read speaks of a life review upon entrance to the other side. Many of those who have had a near-death experience come back with the same story. In Raymond Moody's book,* Life After Life, *he summarizes many reports of a life review from the people he interviewed who had a near-death experience. The common elements were that one's entire life, or major parts of one's life, flashed by in vivid detail. Positive memories as well as moments of regret for causing pain were recalled. Jordan McKay says his review included what he called "failures" in his life, as well as seeing the actual consequences of every choice. So I broached this topic with Frances:]*

C: Was your life review difficult to experience? Some say it's very hard to learn of the pain you caused others during your earth lifetime because you get to feel the pain.

F: Of course it's hard. But it's so necessary. It's part of the learning experience of incarnation. You cause pain because of neglect, or omission. And sometimes direct commission. You get the indelible knowledge of what it feels like and make a vow to never do that again. But you wouldn't, maybe couldn't have learned that without causing it in the first place.

C: Does that life review impact the people who were the recipients of the pain?

F: Yes, indeed. You extend your deepest apologies to them in ways I can't explain. Like telepathy to both incarnate and discarnate beings whom you ask for forgiveness. It all happens very quickly and it's over.

But make no mistake. It's not like a slight burn when you brush something hot. The pain is real, deep, third degree, if that's what it was on earth. But then the episodes of review are over, and you start to make your way into this unspeakably beautiful, rich environment with lots of help from those who love you. Your spirit guides who helped you through your earthly sojourn are now so happy to see you reunited with all the other parts of your greater Self.

C: What have you learned from the Frances Vaughan persona?

F: Love is the answer. I came to know how much love I was capable of and how much it matters within an incarnation. I spread it around as best I could, and made sure I expanded my capacity for love at the same time. I'm realizing that one lifetime is only one lifetime. Use it well. I think I did. I'll be able to do even better next time.

C: Your memorial was certainly a testimonial to that.

F: It was. But people who die without fancy memorials, in the streets, at a concert, etc., are also carriers of Love. Look what's happening to the Parkland kids.* So full of passion for life, for themselves, and most of all for their age peers who want an education and a life that's full of love, not fear. Keeping a gun in a classroom underscores fear. They know that and don't want it.

C: Will you reincarnate?

F: I am incarnated in other forms — people, as well as other "shards" of myself. It's all going on "at the same time." I am learning from all of them. Like sending little pieces of myself to school and they all are reporting back, or rather, feeding into my soul group the lessons and the errors they are learning. My purpose (in the Frances Vaughan incarnation) was to sing the praises of the One, show a way to connect with the One — "transpersonal" was a bit clunky as a word, but it served those of us educated in philosophy and psychology. We're on the cusp. We see ahead to our future state of greater consciousness, but we often don't know how to get from here to there. Jump? Take an arduous route because it's more virtuous? Go round and round on a merry-go-round of spiritual choices, hoping to find one that suits us?

C: How would you describe what you did?

F: I committed myself to learning.

C: What kinds of learning?

F: Compassion is the "biggie," I think. But there are more subtle learnings too, that can be gleaned from your stay on earth.

Recovering a sense of balance when we become incarnate — because we lose a sense of how it all works. The magnificent balance of the universe in its yin/yang oscillations. Landing on earth is a shock, and we also choose to forget where we came from for a while. All of which causes us to lose balance and wobble. Remember that a gym is not only for strength and endurance. It's also simply to learn more deeply the balance needed to push against resistance, not fall forward, not fall backward — all of which can happen and does happen.

Look at a baby learning how to walk. Falls over constantly — get up, fall, hold on, let go, fall. We're babies, learning a finer sense of balance — how to hold onto our inner sense of values while being buffeted by the physical forces of life on earth. The wind can knock you over. Rain can beat you down. Sun can burn you to a crisp — literally. Tough forces here. Not only a moral gymnasium but a physical one that teaches what those beautiful Olympic athletes teach us: that success in their sport is not only the physical skills. It's [also] the mental stamina and determination. More than that, the medal winners know that to "win" you must transcend your own boundaries, whatever you've defined them to be — physical strength, belief in yourself that you can do it, not being afraid to fail, to completely embarrass yourself, not being afraid to die in some sports. The ultimate message is "don't be afraid to die" — physically, mentally, psychologically.

Look at those little girl gymnasts molested by the "team doctor." Horrible! He should be ashamed.* But they were willing to pay *that* price, the price of admission, as it were, to the gymnasts' world in order to compete and possibly win the gold, or die trying.

We asked them ("we" in the collective sense of those who were running the program, watching the practices and competitions), we asked them to endure that assault to their personhood in order to be in the contests that they competed in. What a personal challenge! How many girls dropped out of the program because they wouldn't pay the price? Many. Their moral compass said, "No, I will not surrender to this assault." And that's fine for them. But let's consider the ones who said, "Yes — I will do whatever it takes because I've chosen this arduous path as my own, with all its affronts and indignities. I may be scarred for the rest of my life, or deformed, or disabled in some way, but I'll try this way."

C: Thank you. That was a brilliant piece of insight. What other paths besides sports call upon us to sacrifice ourselves, so to speak? Or accept compromises?

F: Many. You can come up with many if you see it in this frame. Parenting [is one]. [Another is] writing books, and the balance there is "truth vs. popularity" [writing something you know as truth vs. writing something that you know will sell books]. Running an organization honestly without malfeasance or tawdry things like sexual abuse, harassment, and so on. Running a classroom that truly benefits children and isn't merely about gaining a paycheck. The list is endless.

Finding the balance between self and other. What's good for me isn't always the best for you, and vice versa. Balance. The Olympic sports just make it "writ large." That's part of the attraction — they are teachers of balance. Or they're not, and the competitors fail, or worse, die. Football, NASCAR racing, horse racing — all about balance or death (or a kind of death from permanent injury.)

Not necessarily for everyone. Simply a chosen path for some. But ideally we find a way to challenge ourselves and maintain that balance — or not. If not, we take what we've learned into another lifetime. People who incarnate with infirmities or disabilities, who call upon the rest of us to see their suffering, to enlarge our hearts and see the connections to all beings are some of the real gift-givers of the species.

Learning How to Tune In

C: What would you like to focus on today?

F: Quantum physics. *[laughing]* Not exactly. But what it's like to stand outside ordinary [Earth] reality and see a bigger, more detailed picture of how it all works. And I'm just starting to learn this while here.

It's all energy. It's all interacting for better or worse. There's no avoiding it. Even if you were in a cave for months, or years, you would be interacting with the energies that you would reach out to, or that would visit you.

C: How could we benefit from being aware of these energies?

F: You'd be drawn to good ones, positive ones. Avoiding negative energies, places, people that dull your consciousness, that lead you astray from your life purpose.

Always try to "tune in" like a radio to what "frequencies" are around you. Don't assume that because someone looks educated, well-dressed, they are positive. We often get taken in by appearances.

And don't assume that people looking ragtag, lost, even sinister are always negative. Remember the young black man you once saw standing on a corner near Oakland Technical High School? You got it that inside a gruff exterior was a lost boy who wanted to be loved.

We can't "save" everyone we meet, but we can sure send each person a "hello" energy that is positive, loving, a kind of "I see you" energy that honors their connection to the Whole, no matter what their circumstances. Send energy — loving, healing energy — to anyone alive or "dead." They'll receive it, and it will benefit them. We must not give up on anyone.

C: What's to come for those of us caught up in this fear-filled world right now?

F: More fear, I'm afraid. *[smiles at pun]* It will get worse before it gets better. And it will get better. That "moral gymnasium" idea is a useful one. This is quite a workout for many — for example, immigrants without correct papers, teenagers learning about climate change, to name just two. Time to ripen those values, those seeds of love, beauty, joy, justice that so many of us planted in the 20th century. Keep ripening those values. It will contribute to the "collective consciousness," as well as help you evolve individually. Whether our species survives this period is a matter for the dynamics of Earth and our species to work out.

C: Is collective consciousness a valid concept?

F: Yes, it is. There are groupings of souls, beings, who hold shared values and who make daily deposits. Now, this can be those values I mentioned, or values of hatred, greed, murder, violence of all kinds.

Those groupings are strong within themselves. I know you like to think of one collective consciousness — an intermingling of emotions, ideas, and acts, with maybe a merging, softening of the negative by the positive. On a very large scale, maybe so. But what's more pronounced, and more relevant to what's going on now on earth is the separate groupings of kindred spirits. There's not going to be some tremendous Armageddon where these groupings clash, or win the other side over. That's not what earth's about. It's a way station.

An individual grows in consciousness; an oversoul, or a soul group, grows by virtue of member deposits. That's plenty of work for a life on earth. Earth will not see a "new age" where all is utopian. That is not its role. It's doing fine as a moral gym.

I hope you can rest with that.

Soul Work

C: Do we live concurrent lifetimes as "shards" of ourselves, as participants in a soul group?

F: Yes, many times in many ways — too many to imagine. But they do "bleed" into each other — better to say "inform each other." So the one you are aware of — as I was Frances Vaughan and you are Cindy Spring — is the vehicle of your focus of consciousness and what you have to work with. Making it more "tuned in" — seaworthy, so to speak — for the journey toward God or Unity Consciousness is always the task, no matter which "vehicle" you're in. And it benefits all the others at the same time.

It's really impossible to describe how it actually works. So many more dimensions of reality than even our most fertile minds on earth can imagine. Suffice it to say that we are complex beings *in toto*, leading singular lives across a spectrum of time and places. All joined into its own unity — the developmental level of the whole entity.

C: What is maturity in terms of an incarnation on earth?

F: The full flowering of a human being means coming to the realization that you are one with God. Those are my terms. Your focus becomes "soul work." There's no criterion in "maturity" [that calls] for greatness or saintliness or piousness. Just realization of the Oneness of it all.

C: What do you mean by "soul work"?

F: The term is misused and sometimes trivialized in "the new age." It means digging deep into your consciousness and expanding your awareness of energies around you, deeper mysteries of life, partnering with soulmates (you can have more than one).

It's fun to develop physical prowess in something, or do mental gymnastics within the intellect, and so on. But soul work is actually available to everyone. [There's] no need for an athletic body or a high IQ. Just a conscious determination to explore the depth of being you've been given while here on earth. So much territory to explore, so many ways to do it.

C: Such as?

F: Sunshine. Like seeing things on a crystal-clear day in all their glory and detail. Colors. That's what it's like now. I get glimpses of the next phase here. It is "heavenly," but I know now that I could have had those moments on earth. I just didn't let myself have fun very often. Too concerned with contribution and serious intellectual pursuits and the details of life.

C: How can those of us who see "spiritual practices" such as meditating, or reading serious spiritual tomes, allow ourselves to see the other things — the fun — as also contributing much to our evolution?

F: Go inside. See how it makes you feel. Singing great songs that touch your soul and the souls of others. You were singing *Age of Aquarius* today and feeling happy, uplifted. [Vietnamese Buddhist teacher] Thich Nhat Hanh* said, "Look at the rose out the window." The Dalai Lama* says, "Be kind." They know what they're talking about. They get simplicity, the joy in simple things. It's momentary, sure. But it's soul-producing. It expands, deepens that entity we call soul into a larger, more conscious being. Just those little things.

A moment's rest in a lovely site, or a piece of music can do more than hours of meditation. All is Love. What deepens your love of life, of others, of the tiniest detail of a rock or bird is soul-enhancing. Obviously, [there's] hospice work. How deep can you go when you stand at the threshold of death with someone?

Trust your deep knowing that what seems to create more love is always right.

Holding a Larger Frame on Death

C: What insights have you gained about the dying process?

F: Many-faceted. Like turning over a large crystal with many facets to see. All depends on the set of emotions you've gathered. Are you dying with grace, as K. D. Singh* suggests is possible? Beautiful, but very few achieve that without help.

Are you dying in terror of annihilation as your mother-in-law was, and would have, if it had not been for "The Wave and The Drop" story — the gift you gave her? Are you surrounded by loved ones who don't want to let you go? Understandable, but not helpful, or as helpful as they could be if they simply "held you in a circle" instead of projecting their own needs into the situation.

Those of us "on this side" see the folly of holding onto someone who is already on the bridge — crossing the River Styx, if you will — and heading with resolution to this greater reality. They will experience whatever they expect — at first. What opens up for each person after the initial entry depends on who's waiting, what "karma" he or she needs to consider from the life just left. They have a home here, where they left from before they took on earth life, to go to and relax with loved ones.

C: What about committing suicide? How is that held in the greater reality?

F: Most everyone alive on earth still senses that they must fulfill their purpose, their unique purpose. Some give up. Suicide is not immoral. It's giving up on the particular life-time because it's too hard, too many unanticipated road-blocks. The lessons to be gained, outlined before incarnation, will still have to be learned. But in another incarnation, perhaps better structured with more support for success.

C: Where are we in terms of our evolution as a species?

F: About halfway. Consciousness will continue to evolve with or without humans, make no mistake about that. We can contribute as we have, or drop out for other species to take the lead here on this planet. Earth has a *telos* to evolve into fruition as a planet, as an apple does, ripe for plucking and nourishing others. It will do that unless it's blown to smithereens and made uninhabitable. I doubt that will happen. But you never know about free will and where it can take you. It has taken us to some very dark places. But the Light is always calling, always "beckoning unto us," as we told in the story of hell.

We can separate ourselves from God, the Light, Allah, the One — whatever name we give it. But we are always being beckoned back to the enormous Love and Communion being offered to us. "Go to the Light" is a mantra for all of us. That's why candles are so attractive. They call us to the Light, speak to us of one Light that we all share in the greater reality. Amen.

Welcome O Life! I go to encounter for the millionth time the reality of experience, and to forge in the smithy of my soul the uncreated conscience of my race.

— JAMES JOYCE

....

EXERCISE

Question to reader: What is your purpose in being incarnate at this time?

C's answer: My purpose is to learn about and promote a sense of connection with all living beings, with all manifestations of Life in physical forms, in dynamic processes. My hope for our species is that the highest levels of human consciousness — Love, Beauty, Joy, Truth, Justice, Compassion, Wisdom — can be saved and used to begin anew our planet's evolution within the universe we inhabit.

Take the time to write some thoughts on your purpose here.

....

How does one live with the knowledge that there is life after life?

✑

The result of all sincerely followed paths… is a change in consciousness in the one who walks the path. Sometimes gradually, sometimes suddenly, the traveler perceives a previously unseen order and meaning in the universe — a recognition that gives significance to life by merging the boundaries of the self with the cosmos. He recognizes that, paradoxically, the deepest aspect of himself is one with all creation.… It is a state in which there is constant awareness of unity with the universe pervading all aspects of one's life.

— EDGAR MITCHELL, Apollo 14 astronaut, Founder of Institute of Noetic Sciences

When Matthew McKay discovered that he could communicate with his son who was on "the other side," a whole new world opened up for both of them. Matthew was able to have a direct experience of life after life and carry that greater reality within him during this incarnate lifetime. How would it change your life to know, as Matthew says, that *"we are in this together, and we never lose each other? The souls who reincarnate together, life after life, are like a repertory theater company. We have many parts in hundreds of plays, but the circle of love and relationship is never broken. We rejoin in the life between lives to review our work and learn from what we've done."*

In *Seth Speaks,* channeled by Jane Roberts, Seth encourages us to pay attention to stray thoughts rather than dismiss them:

> *"Some of these may involve what* you *would call a reincarnational self, focused in another period of history… according to your psychic suppleness, your curiosity, your desire for knowledge. In other words, you may become aware of a far greater reality than you know now, use abilities that you do not realize you possess, know beyond all doubt that your own consciousness and identity is independent of the world in which you now focus your primary intention."*

This sixth question in our journey together raises two personal questions: (1) How much, or how little, does this expanded consciousness impact our daily choices? (2) How can we use this knowledge to meet the challenges ahead? So let's explore how to live with this knowledge….

C: How does one hold the knowledge of the greater reality while living in "ordinary" reality?

F: Lightly, by bringing Light and Harmony and Love to every situation you can. Your focus while incarnate must be on your physical life and your purpose. Plus working out the unique plan you have for this lifetime — what knowledge, what greater wisdom about the universe and God and Love can you gain?

C: How else does this knowledge impact one's life?

F: As we've been saying, it lessens the fear of death. To live without that knowledge means that you're always fearful that something will happen to you that is bad, painful, scary, and downright abhorrent — [that is], to die. That's the ego's version. And death is the end to that particular form of ego — the persona you cultivated in that lifetime.

But your unique characteristics — your values, sense of humor, way of approaching problems, talents, and what your soul's true essence is, those will carry over to the life-after-life period of your existence. As we discussed earlier, the outer person is like a costume, a set of clothes that fit who you are/were on earth.

[Where I exist], you don't need to *be* something, or pretend you are something you're not. Your true essence is what gets exhibited, and you will be surprised and pleased at how much more wonderful you are than you might have thought. God's love enhances and fills out your being here, and you radiate the joy of being home again.

Another aspect of knowing about death as transition, not end, is a happiness beyond measure. You know that what you're experiencing in this particular lifetime will be over — any sorrow, physical pain, horrible circumstances, loss — all vanish at the instant you are truly dead to earth life and moving toward the Light of this greater dimension.

Unless, of course, you'd prefer to hold onto some remnant of being alive in earth terms — and many souls do — and you become stuck in a limbo which does exist. You are neither here, in a true life between incarnations, nor are you living among the incarnate ones. For those souls we have spirits who offer to help move the person along by getting them to realize they are dead to earth. And many beings of Light and Love are waiting to escort them to their chosen place in the afterlife — or more accurately, the between-lives space.

C: I'm asking myself, and I imagine our readers will want to know too — how does knowing there is "life after life" change our participation in earth life?

F: What is "earth life" but a series of events, emotions, highs and lows — and most often, confusing? Death puts a period on all of that. It's like you writing one of our sentences and coming to a period. While you're writing it, it feels right, good, flowing, but in the back of your mind you know it won't go on and on. The sentence will end.

Another analogy would be an amusement ride. You climb aboard. The Ferris wheel or the roller coaster takes you off and away. But in the back of your mind you know this ride will end. So enjoy it as much as you can, get the thrills of being off balance, high up, or speeding along a curve, but always knowing that the ride will end, no matter how scary or dizzying it is.

Knowing you will die and it won't be a blackout of nothingness will help you recover from bad moments. And if you have the grace to see that there's a dimension of love and welcome and respite on the other side, you'll walk through that doorway so much more easily. Trust me, I know it's so.

C: Did you know that to be the case before you died?

F: I did. But there's always that little bit of doubt, lingering in the shadows, that has its place. Like getting married to a person you love. It seems so right, but there's that "what-if" bird flying in the trees, reminding us that our plans are subject to larger variables, like "Can we grow old together?" Or a sudden death, as in Jordan McKay's case. His father Matthew was devastated.

We are lucky to be breaching this dimension of being while alive, as I was, and as you are. I've had some tough [lifetimes]. You have to [in order] to get anywhere in the development of consciousness. But they don't all have to be pain and suffering. Some do.

C: Can you say more about the impact upon the day-to-day activities, choices one makes, and so on, with the knowledge of the greater reality?

F: Choices are made with the larger frame in mind — "How does the choice further my work while I'm incarnate"? It's not as cut-and-dried as that — meaning, it's not a constant awareness. It's much more subconscious in the sense that it [the choice] "feels right" or seems to lead to a happier, more productive and joyful existence.

Not to say it's all that way [joyful]. Your choice to incarnate in the first place has the understanding that the lessons may be tough, very challenging, with disappointments and even failures along the way. In a good life-plan, that's all built in. Asking yourself, "What am I learning from this — from this loss, from this diagnosis, from this failure?"

The comprehension of a greater reality helps us in those times when things fall apart...

- When we lose a loved one to the other side,
- When we lose our possessions, livelihood, or our community to a crime or disaster,
- When we're losing our own life and walking on the bridge of transition.

That's when knowing we are connected to other dimensions, an omnipresent Ocean of Love, and outside the space/time dimension, comes in handy.

Remember Angeles Arrien's* wonderful questions: "What's learnin' ya today? What's workin' ya?" In other words, what's the teacher that's confronting you today? A boss? A child who is impossible to discipline? A medical challenge? Or maybe someone meting out abuse of some sort that you have to decide how to handle — Speak out? Suffer? Become stronger to be able to resist? There are no right answers to that, by the way. Any response has its built-in reasons for being the best one in the moment.

All to say that living your earth life within a larger matrix of understanding, and even experimentation as to alternative scenarios, is a learning strategy. In a sense there are no wrong answers, wrong responses. Only situations we learn from and move on.

That may seem harsh if [our] choices result in other people's suffering. But there's a way to understand all the machinations of earth life and individual behavior in a field of endless possibilities.

Shakespeare was close to the mark when he wrote: *All the world's a stage, and all the men and women merely players; they have their exits and their entrances, And one man in his time plays many parts....*

It's much more complicated than that, but that viewpoint is a valid one among many.

Life Purpose and Karma

C: What can you say about karmic debt from past or concurrent lifetimes?

F: It's not as simple as [to] do something harmful or hurtful to someone else and have to pay for it later in that lifetime, or in another. Remember the life-review scenario I mentioned [in Question 5, p. 72]? It's part of a larger frame on how we learn from and atone for our errors in judgment, acts that cause pain to others.

At the risk of seeming insensitive, I need to say what is true as I understand it. Earth is a testing ground, and a place to learn lessons that are for our benefit as souls committed to moving toward union with the One. All is viewed from that larger perspective. So terrible-looking acts like mass murders, or torture, or imprisonment of innocent people seem to an incarnate to be wholly unjust and despicable. From the earth perspective of moral values, they *are* wrong. From a larger perspective, they are mistakes to be experienced by the perpetrator, who will get to experience the same pain as the victim did. The lesson — that [certain] behavior does not lead to [experiencing] God's Love — becomes indelibly etched in the learner's soul.

C: Are the people we see on a daily basis who are clearly suffering, who are homeless, or in physical or mental pain, and so on, experiencing that lesson of how it feels from the recipient's side?

F: No. Most often the really sad and miserable people who populate your world — and the number seems to be growing — are riding the waves of their game plan, their purpose, their point on their journey. Of course, there are people who are suffering because of their own bad choices — drugs, or exploitive behavior toward others, or shutting down on letting love enter their lives. It's a case-by-case situation. Unless you've developed highly intuitive or psychic skills, you won't be able to tell why someone is in that kind of predicament.

Always be kind, be generous, don't judge. That person will one day die and move on to a greater reality where all this will be sorted out. You can look upon anyone as a teacher, no matter what the circumstance.

C: There's a wonderful bit of wisdom from Hinduism that suggests doing just that — "This is my teacher in a distressing disguise." I use it often, especially when I encounter someone who's disturbing-looking in some way.

F: Yes, you could take most anybody and find the truth of that.

C: Can you say more about life purpose?

F: Each person plans an overall game plan, if you will, for an incarnation. I planned for the person who became Frances Vaughan a soft entry into an upper-middle-class family in California. I was white, female, intelligent, and pretty. In other words, I chose to have a lot of factors welcomed by the dominant culture.

Along the way, I had to choose a career, a husband, whether to have children or not, and so on. All of that came to pass in general terms. But I had free will at every step of the way. My purpose included becoming a teacher of greater consciousness for as many people as cared to follow my offerings. At one point, my marriage to my children's father came apart. Later, my life with Roger* began and was so much more conducive to my sense of who I wanted to be. His support along the way resulted in a much greater fulfillment of my life plan than if I had simply gotten divorced or married someone else. I'll let my memorial, with his lovely tribute to who I was and my work, speak for itself. It was a grand life.

Someone else may choose a game plan that involves poverty or other hardship. Or, for instance, being a dark-skinned person in America, where there's still virulent racism. Every day could contain some insult or injury. But what a challenging circumstance to learn what directed hatred and violence does to a human being — from the receiving end. And how to maintain your dignity as a divine being.

I think every oversoul contains many brave souls who bring that information to the collective understanding. By seeing or experiencing hatred such as racism in its ugliness, that guides the wisdom of the Whole toward the Love of God. It becomes easier for each part of the oversoul to grow in compassion and develop deeper ties of communion. It's all in service to moving toward the One.

Challenges Ahead

C: What else would you like to share this evening?

F: Something big is going to eclipse the turmoil that is gripping the U.S. right now in the drama unfolding around the president. He's a *symptom*, not a cause. I know that's hard to swallow because of his callousness. But it will be swept away by a much more challenging set of circumstances that will test the mettle of those who are prepared to "meet their maker," to use an old term.

Many people will be asked to lay their lives on the line to address some very horrible and tragic events. That is why it is so important to get out the message that death is a transition. It's OK, not easy, but OK to lose your life — your current incarnation — especially in service to a greater ideal. You may be surprised at how many people will be willing to do that, including you.

Knowing that you've died many times and [that you] simply enter into a greater reality where the pain and tragedy are over, and seeing the greater purpose of that period of history, will be comforting. It will be essential for many who might waver or fall back into self-centered survival. You won't. Neither will [your husband]. It is easier for older people, since they've lived out a good deal of their purpose. But you'll see millions of young people choosing death before they compromise their values, much as soldiers who thought they were fighting for freedom and country. Only this time it will be for the World.

C: What is necessary to focus on as we experience the turmoil of our space/time dimension — specifically, life on earth at this moment, with its daily stresses for so many?

F: Patience. So many want to "do something" — make it better, stop the violence, alleviate the pain or "Stop Trump." Trump will stop himself. Sometimes it's better to "hold the circle,"* as you say. I'm not advocating that people in politics or in extremely stressful situations like DACA* stop what they're doing. All necessary. But this book is not for them. It's for people like you [Cindy], like I was when I was alive in body. People of the so-called "higher consciousness" who sense something deeper is called for beyond "action."

C: What does that deeper response look like?

F: Never-ending. Go to a place, a vantage point where you can see [that] the challenges of living on earth will continue. It's supposed to be that way. When challenges were mainly of survival — that was the way it was. Now higher stakes. Growth of soul is called for. Not different really than survival, because we don't "die" in the ordinary sense. It's always been about expanding consciousness.

What we know now — and I'm clearer on it because of my vantage point in the "extraphysical" — is that it's all about Love, about moving toward the Deity and experiencing a greater and greater sense of Oneness. We go by stages: Bonding with one other. Bonding with a group such as a family. Bonding with our soul group. Always expanding our "Oneness." All the rest are details. It means learning to move with greater energy, with more authority.

Call it by whatever name — God, Allah, Deity, the One — it's what those of us on this side and some on your side sense as the divine within, and being within the divine at the same time.

C: What does that look like — the practice of moving toward the One — on a daily basis?

F: Presence in each moment, like the Buddhists talk about. But they often forget to have fun. Recognizing that the world is full of suffering, and trying to move to a larger way of holding it, is work. But no one would choose to incarnate on earth if there wasn't beauty to take in, love to make, events to witness such as births, deaths, marriages. Celebration is a good balance to suffering even in terrible times. Look at the many stories of marriages in Iraq during the war there. Sometimes marriage parties were blown up by bombs. Doesn't stop them from having them. They know how important, how bonding those rituals are, especially in times of violence, chaos, and even death.

The earth is soaked in the blood of countless species. It is also home to countless more who are thriving while they can.

C: What else besides being in the present moment? And rituals?

F: Service. I talked about it some earlier. One-to-one service. The need to serve, just like other needs like food and water and sex and safe homes. We all need safe harbors to rest from the chaos, and we come together to create them for each other. Respond now to others' pain. Your own, as you share or experience it. The "news" you have gotten about this greater reality will be very useful in navigating the upheavals to come.

C: How can we prepare ourselves for worse things to come?

F: You can't really. Oh, you can make emergency kits for immediate problems. But we each have to meet adversity as it shows up. Be creative if we can, and surrender if we must. Remember, we don't die. We drop our bodies with a fond farewell, if we can. We go on to greater awareness. And some rest.

C: What are the ways that incarnate individuals can hold/ tolerate/witness the events of our time with the gargantuan challenges we seem to be facing?

F: We have only to hold it all in Love. I know that may sound simplistic or dismissive of what you're trying to say, but it's the only answer. To increase our capacity for love, for compassion, for gratitude to be alive at this time with the intelligence and resources to respond to suffering is a gift. Use it. Know that your service during this time is not only needed, but expected. You set that expectation for yourself — if you are incarnate now — before you were born.

That's not everyone's role, certainly. But [there's] enough of a cohort of souls who can make the passage easier — the "first responders," as you call them. They've been training many lifetimes for this particular lifetime's challenge. You are all as prepared as you can be.

You cannot stop what's coming. It's been set up as a harmonic rebalance, set in motion by forces larger than just humans on earth. Other species have run their cycle too and are ready to move on.

C: What do we gain by trying to address injustice, or suffering, or violent behavior that kills seemingly innocent people, if it all is meant to happen in some way?

F: Understand that these are lessons. Our responses teach us much — *how* we respond, *what* motivates it, *when* do we give up, and *why*? All of those valuable lessons about the role of consciousness are forged within the soul of the person now facing those challenges. We're all in this together, don't you see? It is an orchestration that demands our best, highest selves. What do *you* want to have happen?

C: I don't know — mitigate the pain, have people know how loved they are by their soul groups in other dimensions. Stop the craziness that seems to be enveloping our world.

F: All that is doable if you are willing to pay the price of [having] greater consciousness when it evolves, as it will, into another form of existence [life after life].

C: Whose consciousness? Mine or the species' collective consciousness?

F: Both. They are inseparable. You have evolved in this particular lifetime to ask questions about "a greater reality." Not many of your associates are doing that. But in a sense, it's not necessary to be asking. It's only necessary to be "being," as it were. Being someone who wants to address the inequities of your world, including cruel torture by humans against other species. When you recognize all that is going on, you want to yell STOP! You want to point out in as many ways as possible how unjust and really ignorant are attitudes of greed and hatred for others. That's because you have reached that level of consciousness, do you see? [smile] You see and feel the pain.

C: I can barely contain any of it. One six-year-old autistic boy who gets lost in a woods, found dead, makes me cry.

F: Bravo! You can also see, if you look, 150 volunteers searching for days, trying to find him. The mother in such pain on TV. We all feel her agony. So much to learn, so much demonstration of how to respond. The little boy was welcomed by many loving guides. He is doing well, missing his parents, but knowing that his suffering as an autistic child in a scary world is over.

"I've begun to glimpse the greater inner dimensions from which our usual lives emerge, and to familiarize myself with other alternate methods of perception that can be used not only to see other 'worlds,' but help us deal more effectively with this one."

— JANE ROBERTS from her Introduction to
The Nature of Personal REALITY/ A SETH BOOK

. . . .

EXERCISE

Try to commit to this awareness for a week. Whenever you encounter a person who you find annoying or rude, or who makes you uncomfortable, say to yourself three times: This is my teacher in a distressing disguise. Not to dismiss the behavior, but to learn from it.

. . . .

Where is Home?

≈

We're all just walking each other home.

— RAM DASS, SPIRITUAL TEACHER

The word *Home* resonates deeply within us. It contains the same sound as the Sanskrit symbol/sound OM. To utter the sacred sound OM is said to call forth ultimate consciousness. *Home* in most of the (English-based) channeled sources refers to a home locale, beyond the space/time dimension, where one's group soul resides.

We must keep in mind that references to a location are only to help us get an image. There is no "place" in outer space, for instance, where groupings of souls reside. But the frequent mentions of "going home" and "being at home" tell us it's a pattern across the various channeled sources. Psychologist Matthew McKay asked his son Jordan the question: "When do we get to join with all the people we love?" Jordan, from his vantage point on the other side, answered:

> When we leave time and return to the spirit world, the illusion of aloneness and loss ends. As soon as possible, we reunite with loved ones. While there is a vast network of billions of souls, we actually live in small communities.

Jordan goes on to explain that, as on earth, we tend to congregate with those who have similar perspectives. In his terms, "we hang with our buddies." At another point he tells us:

> [Earth] is not our home. A physical environment isn't natural to us, and this planet is definitely an acquired taste. There are countless planets — most easier than this one — where souls learn. None of them is home.... Our home is a nonphysical place where we live together, connected by one gravitational force — love.

In the book *Nosso Lar* (*Our Home*), Francisco Xavier channels a story of a doctor, Andre Luiz, who arrives after death in a beautiful setting where many souls share an earth-like existence that is a way station for rehabilitation. He meets many souls who did not make the most of their incarnation and, like him, focused on accumulation of wealth and self-centered pursuits. The rehab environment is staffed by loving and wise people who provide a recovery process and spiritual education that's supervised by more evolved spirits.

After an extended stay in rehab, Andre Luiz is released to move on to active learning. He remarks, *"Until now, I had lived in Nosso Lar as a sickly guest in a shiny palace. I had been so entirely wrapped up in myself that I was incapable of perceiving its enchantment and marvels."* He goes on to learn skills in order to be of service to the incarnate ones on earth.

Sister Frances Banks tells us that she attended her own memorial service (in spirit), and then, *"I relaxed into peace. Life goes on for me now on a fuller and more abundant scale of living. I am living in the Rest Home, though I am now occupying a 'cottage' of my own. It is a lovely little place.... I still belong to the Home of course, and I go back there frequently."* For Sister Frances, the "Rest Home" was the place where other nuns of her order who had passed from their earth incarnation now lived together and continued their work "on the other side."

Taken as a whole, what these entities are telling us is that *Home* is primarily a divine creation. Our *Home* in the afterlife is the model for our attempts during incarnations to make a place where we can live and share ourselves with all our heart and soul.

C: How would you describe "home" in the greater reality?

F: Home is where your soul group stays to "keep the hearth" (and heart) going. It's not on earth or any dimension near earth. It can have a consensus or shared architecture that's earth-like or not. But other members don't all necessarily have earth incarnations.

It's a place of deep bonding, deeper learning for all of us to share. I went to my soul group to share what I learned as Frances Vaughan. Some members were beyond the Frances Vaughan level, and yet were very interested in the particulars of my experience.

C: Why is that?

F: Because each lifetime is creatively unique and therefore has an aesthetic or informational value that only that personality of mine can describe.

We all like to see different colors, hear different sounds. It's much more than a simple aesthetic experience on earth. Here the stories can bring beautiful Light, increase the Love we share. All in service to Communion. It also offers ideas for incarnations to those who haven't had quite the circumstances I created and danced in, so to speak.

Life is a dance on so many levels. Dancing to different beats with different partners in so many contexts. All in service to the self, to the earth community, and to the much larger community we connect with here. Home is what it sounds like — a place to rest, to enjoy relationships, and make plans.

C: What kinds of plans?

F: How we can develop our existing personalities — the ones who populate our unique souls — in order to correct past mistakes and steer things in a better direction than what we know happens in the so-called future. It's all happening at once, but those of us with a more limited set of awarenesses can only focus on one, or at best, a few at a time. [Through the channeling of this book] I wanted to share with others in the physical dimension that we remain very much alive. There are some memories and events which can fade a bit if we choose them to do so. But [from where I am], we can see all of our lives, all of our memories, all of our events simultaneously. I'm putting this all in terms you and our reader can understand. It is so much more expansive, expanded, beyond human experience.

Every Dimension You Can Imagine, and Then Some

C: I'm concerned that we might come off as too "new agey" with our Love/Light scenarios. Aren't there dark parts to the greater reality?

F: Of course. But not where you might think. Not all around us as in a dark, threatening forest. Not like in a homeless encampment, where danger is everywhere because people are desperate. There is no desperation here, no feeling of foreboding that something bad might happen. It's all Love, Gratitude, Joy of being with God, or the One. But it's much more differentiated than the old heaven or nirvana stories. It's infinitely diverse. If you want danger, you can create it. But it's like the dangers of a video game. How dangerous is that? You can have the "thrill" of predator/prey, but it's a game. You always know it's a game, as you do on earth.

C: How are you this evening?

F: Fractured by the events going on in your world, with more fracture and dislocation to come. And I'm enjoying the beautiful simplicity of "life after life," with all its splendor and omnipresent love. It's not escapism to want to visit and learn about this greater reality while you're incarnate. It's good to keep the inquiry open-ended and reflective, however.

We all come from here — some incarnate on earth, some elsewhere — and we each return home when we're called, or decide that the lifetime is complete, or too hard, or too off-track (like the people addicted to opioids).

Becoming one with the multi-dimensional reality beyond earth reality is what we yearn for, even if you don't realize it. It's Rumi's reed, made into a flute, wanting to return to the mud flat.

I am watching you grow in understanding, comprehension of the Unity of all dimensions, and trying to balance that with all the fractured and fracturing world you're living in. I don't envy you. You are being drawn to good teachers, good materials, and good practices — like this writing — that are serving you and will serve a larger audience. It's not easy, but on the other hand, you can't stop. You'd be so miserable if you gave up this quest.

C: I know that's true. What about my concern that we will come off as too "heavenly" or as too grand or glossy about "the other side?"

F: It's much more grand and glossy than you can imagine. We will not overstate its wonder. We will understate it, because words are not available.

Calling Home

C: What are ways to connect with loved ones on the other side?

F: Just say the word. By that I mean you can connect anytime you want to by invoking the person's name, or calling out: "Hello, are you there?" while holding their image or feeling you have for that person. It's all telepathic. The message/vibration reaches immediately. There's no time lag or space lag. You have to be in a receptive mode. Be open. Be seated or standing still, and ready to give full attention to the conversation.

Eventually you'll develop an easy dialogue, but the first few times may be bumpy. Getting the channel open. Getting rid of doubt that this could actually happen. It does! All the time. So many people connecting with loved ones.

C: I've heard that a mother/child connection is very powerful, especially if the child has died tragically.

F: Yes. That's a channel ripe for communication. Another is mother/daughter at any stage of life. When that relationship has been close on earth, it remains so in the next dimension, as well as across dimensions.

C: Do family members who emotionally hold onto a dying person delay that person's moving on?

F: Not necessarily. It may seem so to the observer. But don't forget that these people with their bonds of love are connected on other levels as well. All the "pieces" of the family are aware of what's going on. The dying person wants to hold on too. Why not, when you're receiving so much love and attention?

Eventually, the body wears out. Or the pain is too great, or the uselessness of holding on becomes clear and it's time to go. As we've heard many times from those who work in hospice settings, a dying person often leaves when no one is around. Makes a clean getaway.

There's a pull from the other side too. [From] loved ones who have passed on, not only from this lifetime, but from others you've shared as well. They're waiting on the other side and have their emotional signals as well.

This is an Ocean of Love. The beings I know here have loved ones, or pieces of themselves still incarnate. They have a mother's concern, but also want to give incarnate beings on earth their time in the "gymnasium." We are watching carefully. Your work as a "first responder" is going well. But that will be for the many who die in the process that you are all experiencing. We want to preserve the human species as one species among many, as you so well put it in your talk. *

We are certain some humans will prevail. What numbers and in what character mode [level of consciousness development], we don't know. At least *I* don't from my consciousness at this point.

....

EXERCISE

Sit still, center yourself in the present moment. Take the question: "Where is home for me?" Answer it with whatever comes to mind. Let your answers just come. They can be trite, or silly, or get outside our dimension. If you stay with this exercise for at least 10-15 minutes, you'll find your answers coming from deeper and deeper in your psyche. Write your answers down, or record them. I did it and a friend recorded my answers. This is well worth the effort.

....

As an example, here are some of my answers:

C: Where is home for me?

A place to be safe, to carry on ordinary aspects of life, for continuity, for order in one's life, to have fun.

A place to invite friends, to do jigsaw puzzles, watch basketball games, make love, play with cats, listen to music, where I order my world; where I'm in charge (to a certain extent).

A place where I can reflect on who I am; where I can work on contributions I think I can make; a place of lovingkindness; a place to invite friends to share food, to share deeper bonds of friendship, where Charlie and I share our soulmate relationship; a place to thrive, a symbol of Home and stability for those whose home does not provide as much stability.

[deeper]

A place that is not carnivorous, where plants thrive, people thrive. A safe place to think, a refuge for reading and writing as an expression of who I am and what I hope to accomplish.

A place where I have a cosmology, a whole story that I can say feels like home; like joining a community, a shared perspective, a place of belonging.

Eden — a place to be happy, a place of plentitude, no strife, paradise.

Where I can embrace the world the way it is.

A vegan planet.

Where all the people I love are in one place.

This Earth where I came out of and will return to and am entirely connected to in the space/time dimension.

Home is in the air, in the water.

Home is in my Heart. [When this came, it felt like a break-through to my truest answer.]

[Note: Having done this exercise and pondering the answers very consciously, I feel that by using my heart as a compass, a directional guide, I can judge the usefulness of any contemplated action, can sense the "rightness" of a situation, and can stop worrying about whether I should be doing something I'm not doing, and so letting go of guilt. I found home in my heart.]

Parting Thoughts

C: Frances, can you give us some closing thoughts?

F: What can be said at this point is...

Shalom — peace be with you

Namaste — I recognize and honor the divine within you

Auf Wiedersehen — till we meet again in the greater reality

We are so elementary in our understanding of this "greater reality" dimension — I mean me too. I hope I've given our readers a glimpse of my reality and some of what I know to be true about it. It's immense and I'm still a stranger in paradise. But having you as the channel to begin to convey what's known about life after life is a gift to us all.

I'm learning what it means to be rejoined with my soul group — dear ones I've known forever, it seems. Yet I'm so novice in my awareness of how it all works.

C: What do you hope our readers will take with them from this brief encounter with a greater reality — through this portal of automatic writing?

F: I see them moving into their lives with more confidence in their being more than a temporal being. To live as an immortal soul while doing the tasks of an earth incarnation is a wonder. It gives nobility, majesty, to what may seem like an "ordinary" life. You are god-like. You contain a connection to a divine realm that is guaranteed, bona fide, as true as anything ever said about divinity.

You may have chosen a humble garb for this incarnation, but don't be fooled! You are divine — a part of a timeless and limitless expanse of being, with many other aspects to yourself not part of your earthly person, but nonetheless a greater being, who let out a shard of itself into the dense matter of earth for a learning, a chance to create something unique for all of us.

Don't waste it! It took eons to get yourself to this incarnation. Show that you know yourself as a Light for others, infusing them with your glorious divinity. Not in any kind of egotistical way. That would backfire badly. By deed, by kindness, by love in so many ways — anything you choose to do — infuse it with Light and Love and make it a beacon for others.

The world you inhabit badly needs more Light, more warmth of love and interconnection. Those of you, having read this book, are getting a glimpse of your conscious awareness. It tells you there's more to life than material stuff, more than how many friends you have, or how many non-profits you support.

Live a singular life that you and the rest of us can be proud of. Live it with gratitude every day that you are a divine spark in a darkening world. Just as each day has a sunrise and sunset, so too do lives and epochs. There's a setting sun on the horizon.

Just as Tagore said: The lamp can be put out because the dawn has come. [Now] it is time to relight the lamp — your being — because darkness is setting in again, and there's work to be done in the recesses of our minds and hearts while a dark night passes. But as we know, and count on, the dawn comes and with it the promise of a new day and a way to live our incarnations with the joy of knowing that whatever shows up, we've chosen that challenge — to meet it, to love it, and to die by it if necessary. It's all part of the lesson, you know.

My final thought to our readers is the first one we gave you — Death is a transition to another form of existence. If you get that one, you'll live with much less fear, much more of a sense of participation in a grand performance called life on earth. Let your star shine!

Epilogue

by Cynthia Spring

Frances summed up our work together on Book One* by underscoring its theme: "Death is a transition to another form of existence." She and I have already begun work on Book Two, which will be a deeper look at some of the same questions. But it's important to acknowledge the human (space/time) side of existence and why we do have a fear of death. In my book *The Wave and The Drop: Wisdom Stories about Death and Afterlife*, I expressed it like this:

> *Fear of death is normal. It's instinctive — watch any predator/prey encounter. All animals, including humans, react with fear when threatened.... The sense of an ending deepens our appreciation of the present moment, our sense of the preciousness of our existence. When we are deeply aware of own mortality, we live with more compassion for others, more awareness of the beauty and sorrow around us, and more freedom from the fear of our own day of passing on.*

How to balance the "wired-in" fear of death with the knowledge of a greater reality is for each of us to figure out.

Getting to Here

During the dialogue sessions with Frances, I was *Here* and she was *There*. That bridge became easier and easier to cross. I can see in retrospect how I was gradually incorporating *There* into *Here*. My *experience* of a greater reality happened whenever *Here* included *There*. One day, the bridge collapsed, and the two sides merged into *Here*. It felt like I'd moved into much more spacious living quarters where Frances and I found we could share, in the *Here* and *Now*, a spacious palace of many rooms.

When the *Here/There* Bubble popped, I began experiencing the reality of All That Is — as much as I can glimpse and take in. Physical reality permeates it but does not dominate. For longer and longer periods, it's all *Here*. This has helped considerably to address the imbalance I was feeling during that first year of automatic writing: Am I *Here* or am I *There*? Some days were very wobbly. I really had to pay attention to the ground rules of the dimension I was in — space/time. I still do!

At this point, the sense of linear time or physical space doesn't exert an absolute grip on my experience. Yes, I'm most often living in *Here*, not *There*. The hypnotic program of materiality is way too strong. But once in a while, when I'm *Here*, it includes Frances, my dad, my spirit guides, and other members of my community, incarnate and discarnate. It's a home that includes a greater reality.

Believing and Knowing

People have asked me why I'm so committed to learning about "the greater reality." I've answered that I want to be able to say with utmost authenticity: "I know it because I've experienced it." While I've been on this journey to direct experience, I've studied and admired many whom I saw as Teachers. Richard Bach inspired millions of us to fly on the wings of Jonathan Livingston Seagull. Through subsequent books, he shared his out-of-body experiences. Huston Smith studied, wrote about, and practiced some of the world's major religions. When asked near the end of his life to comment on death he said, "There is no such thing. It doesn't exist." Of course, I am indebted to Joseph Campbell, who was interviewed by Bill Moyers in the PBS series *The Power of Myth*. In the segment "The Masks of Eternity," Moyers asked, "Is a divinity just what we think?" Campbell answered, "Yes!" Then Moyers asked, "But what does that do to faith?" Campbell replied, "I don't have to have faith. I have *experience*."

Other Teachers of mine have lives that reflect a deep connection to All That Is. Jane Goodall, through her work in Africa creating conservation refuges that intertwine animals with people in villages, has taught me: "It's all connected." Psychologist Jean Houston exhorted me to stretch myself to become "the possible human" by consciously participating in my own evolution. One more I'll mention — Jane Roberts. She had the skill and the courage to channel Seth, thus creating a set of books that remains one of our best maps of the "greater reality." It's from Jane that I learned the term.

The mantra of my writing persona has been: "If you can't say it simply, you don't understand it well enough," attributed to Albert Einstein. Remember, he gave us $E = mc^2$ that explained all of physical reality. That was until quantum physics came along to show that this equation covered only part of the picture. Now we have a larger frame that includes non-local consciousness.

So I encourage you to pop those bubbles. Don't confine yourself to a limited dimension. Expand your consciousness to include nonmaterial realities. Choose a portal through which to explore the greater realities, and commit to it. But be sure to stay grounded in our familiar space/time dimension. That's where you'll find stability and fulfill the purpose of this lifetime. Use well the time you have left.

Please know and appreciate that what Frances and I have presented in *Seven Questions* is our best attempt to "say it simply." This material has been, and will be, superseded by the words of others who grasp more, and who can hold our hand as we walk farther into the hidden reaches of the greater reality. That may not happen while we are in our current incarnations. Spirit guides and loved ones are waiting patiently for us to arrive, in due time, to the "balcony" where we can see farther, broaden our understanding, and learn more.

May you have the thrill of experiencing *There* while you are *Here*. If not this time, then next time. Keep your inner eyes on the prize: union with the One.

I am much more than my physical body. I exist as a soul within a group soul in a greater reality.

I know that my expanded consciousness exists in a beautiful reality of Light and Love and Communion.

The divine is within me. I am within the divine.

I can access the greater reality through my portal of choice, which is …

My purpose for taking on this incarnation known as [your name] is to …

When I recognize that I exist within a greater reality that includes space/time, it allows me to let go of the fear of death.

I am fulfilling my purpose here, and when it's time to go, I will return home.

Automatic writing is the ability to produce written words via telepathy without deliberate conscious thought. The person doing the writing receives whole thoughts from a source outside themselves — perhaps a deceased relative, spouse, or friend — or even a complete stranger. To the receiver, it feels like taking dictation. The receiver writes it out in their own hand or types it on a keyboard.

Channeling is the practice of entering a meditative or trancelike state in order to receive messages from a spiritual guide or other discarnate being. The messages can be written, as in automatic writing, or simply spoken by the channeler. When a channeler assumes a voice, speech patterns, or the personality of the source, they are more often termed a "medium."

Cosmology is the study of how the physical universe came into existence and how it works.

Discarnate means a person or entity not presently (or ever) in a human body.

Incarnate, as a noun, refers to a soul living in a body; as a verb, to incarnate means to take on a lifetime in a body.

Lifetimes: Multiple lifetimes of the same entity. Viewed from within a linear space/time reality, they are perceived as individual, past, present, or future. Viewed from beyond space/time they are perceived as happening simultaneously.

Near-Death Experience (NDE) is a term coined by Dr. Raymond Moody, in his book *Life After Life* (1976). It refers to a person being conscious despite having been declared clinically dead, i.e., having no respiration, heartbeat, or detectable brain wave activity. A person who experiences an NDE later returns to physical life and describes a variety of experiences. These may include observation of their own physical body or the physical environment from an external vantage point. Many accounts contain some version of traveling to a nonphysical environment filled with light and love.

Often the experiencer reports not wanting to return to their body and/or being given a choice of returning, or not. But return they did, eager to describe their own view of heaven and the afterlife. Those who tell their NDE stories in books say that they have a deeper appreciation of life and a greatly diminished fear of death.

Non-local consciousness means awareness and volition not connected with, or dependent upon, a body or brain and therefore independent of space and time. In the realm of non-local consciousness, communication has no boundaries and is instantaneous. Aspects of quantum physics demonstrate a similar independence from normal space and time.

Out-of-Body Experience (OBE) is a term was coined by parapsychology researcher Charles T. Tart in the early 1970s to describe reports from people who said they left their physical bodies and were able to see, hear, and move about in another kind of body, as well as in nonphysical dimensions of reality. Prior to this term, which came to be the most popular one, this phenomenon was called *astral travel* or *spiritual travel*. Tart worked with Robert Monroe, who described his OB experiences in three books, beginning in 1971. (*See Source References*)

Oversoul is defined in the transcendentalism of Ralph Waldo Emerson as a spiritual essence or vital force in the universe in which all souls participate and that therefore transcends individual consciousness. In the books by Jane Roberts channeling Seth, the word "oversoul" is used in a narrower sense of a grouping of souls who incarnate individually and share the learnings of that incarnation with the others upon return Home. This is also referred to as **Group Soul**.

Remote Viewing (RV) is the direct psychic perception of an aspect of the physical world without the use of normal physical senses. In people with well-developed RV talent, time and distance are not barriers to perception. Many parapsychology researchers have written about RV experiments, including Russell Targ, Stephan Schwartz, and Charles T. Tart.

> *"Being psychic is simply being more sensitive to the sea around us. It's simply a method that allows for an additional sense of being."* — Joe McMoneagle, army officer and remote viewer for the CIA during 1980s. From his book *Mind Trek*, p. 113.

Space/Time is a way of representing the four-dimensional reality that we inhabit. Putting the words together as a unit better illustrates the unity we usually experience.

Soul Group is a term used for an individual soul which expresses itself in a variety of ways, including an expression within three-dimensional reality. That physical expression is not by any means the entire soul. It is a fraction of the soul or a shard that participates as one source of information and creativity for the whole soul. In *Seven Questions*, we use Soul Group to indicate one soul with many subselves. **Group Soul** refers to a collection of souls who exist together and often share incarnate lifetimes together. In the channeling literature, these terms are sometimes used interchangeably.

Spirit guides are individual souls who were assigned, or have chosen, to provide guidance, assistance, and protection to an incarnate being during his or her lifetime. They may also help in the transition from physical life to the afterlife.

Tarot is an ancient divination tool that uses a deck of 78 cards to provide guidance for life's questions. Each card contains symbols that capture experiences within human existence. There are many different decks and books for interpretations, but most conform to the original format of 22 Major Arcana cards, and then four suits (cups, wands, swords, and pentacles) of 14 cards each. Both Frances and Cynthia have used this tool for several decades.

Please be aware that these terms and definitions are words on a page, not the reality that is beyond our comprehension.

Endnotes

Aids in reading text: References to people or events in the text that are noted with an * can be found here in the Endnotes.

Full details on sources are listed in **Source References** section.

Introduction

"Yet ultimately..." from *The Coming of Seth,* by Jane Roberts, (Pocket Books, 1976), p. xiii.

"For many years..." from *The Way Back to Paradise,* by Joseph Felser, Ph.D., pp. 201-202.

Carl G. Jung was a Swiss psychiatrist and author who contributed to many fields of inquiry in the 20th century. He can truly be called an explorer of the greater reality.

Lawrence LeShan quote from his essay "Psychic Phenomena and Mystical Experience," in *Psychic Exploration*, an anthology edited by Edgar Mitchell, pp. 572-573.

Emerson quote taken from *One Mind* by Larry Dossey, M.D., on p. xxxiv.

Question 1

Reference to Death/Rebirth card in tarot. Both Frances and Cynthia found tarot cards an excellent tool for guidance. See *The Tarot Handbook* by Angeles Arrien in **References**.

"Parkland kids" reference is to those high school students who experienced a mass shooting at their school, Marjory Stoneman Douglas High School, on Feb. 14, 2018, in Parkland, Florida. They went on to organize protests, voter registration drives, and many other activities. They galvanized students across the country.

"So this is death!..." from *Testimony of Light,* by Helen Greaves, p. 16.

Question 2

(Opening quote) *"If you identify..."* The Nature of Personal Reality, by Jane Roberts, p. 177.

"There is a swelling..." from *Testimony of Light*, by Helen Greaves, p. 116.

"...concurrent, simultaneous..." This is spoken from the perspective of outside of our space/time dimension. Other time references such as "upcoming upheavals" are from the perspective of linear, space/time reality. It's difficult for most of us to maintain both perspectives. It's an evolving awareness that improves with familiarity with this kind of material.

Willis Harman was a professor of electrical engineering at Stanford University and later went on to be the president of the Institute of Noetic Sciences until his death in 1997. He is quoted by friends as saying on his deathbed, "I'm off to my next great adventure."

Coleen Elgin is a nationally recognized video producer with a focus on transformation and spiritual growth. Frances and Coleen were close friends during Frances's lifetime. Coleen produced a beautiful tribute to Frances that was shown at her memorial.

George McMullen had an extraordinary talent for remote viewing. He was involved in working with the CIA during the Cold War, and later with Stephan A. Schwartz in his "intuitive archeology" research. McMullen helped locate the lost Library of Alexandria in Egypt and the bones of Alexander the Great. Mc Mullen died in 2008.

Question 3

(Opening quote) "Nowhere have I encountered...." *The Afterdeath Journal of an American Philosopher*, by Jane Roberts as channeled from William James, p. 162.

The recognition of God... from *Accept this Gift,* Vaughan/ Walsh, p. 92.

Bob Monroe was founder of The Monroe Institute and wrote three books on his out-of-body experiences. See **References** for listing of his books.

Reference to Parkland shooting. See second question in **Endnotes**.

Reference to "saturated solution," a term from chemistry that can be extrapolated into a metaphor that means that a situation has "dissolved" all the input it can, and now that input will not disappear but remain visible.

(Closing quote) *Ask intensely* — from *Desert Wisdom,* by Neil Douglas-Klotz, p. 185.

Question 4

(Opening quote) *"Intuition allows..."* from *Awakening Intuition,* by Frances Vaughan (1979), p. 4.

"I had a heart attack..." as found in *Life After Life,* by Raymond Moody, Jr., p. 76.

For full details on Mary Neal's book *To Heaven and Back: A Doctor's Extraordinary Account of Her Death, Heaven, Angels and Life Again: A True Story,* see **References.**

Reference to remote-viewing. See **Glossary**.

The I Ching is a Chinese divination approach using coin tosses that create a hexagram of 6 lines. Sixty-four different ones are possible. The one the questioner gets that day is the answer or guidance needed.

"Parlor tricks" refers to demonstrations of psi abilities using telepathy or remote viewing. These abilities can be acquired by people who simply want to impress others. Psi abilities are not guarantees to understanding the "greater reality," unless you pursue the larger consciousness from which they derive.

Exercise from *Awakening Intuition*, by Frances Vaughan, p. 22.

Question 5

(Opening quote) *"Physical existence..."* from *Seth Speaks,* p. 82.

Stafford Betty is a professor of religion at California State University at Bakersfield. He has written several books on afterlife and paranormal studies. This quote is taken from his book *Heaven and Hell Unveiled,* p. 35.

"I am aware too..." Greaves/Banks, p. 107.

"...acquire an understanding..." Francisco Xavier/Andre Luiz, in *Nosso Lar,* p. 10.

"The purpose of matter..." *Seeking Jordan,* by Matthew McKay, p. 83.

Reference to Larry Nassar, who was a girls' gymnastics doctor at Michigan State University. He was accused and convicted of molesting hundreds of girls in his care. He's in prison serving a life sentence.

Thich Nhat Hanh and the Dalai Lama are both Buddhist teachers in different lineages.

Reference to Kathleen Dowling Singh, author of *The Grace in Dying* and other fine books.

(Closing quote) James Joyce quote taken from a secondary source — *The Courage to Create* by Rollo May, p. 20. James Joyce was born in 1882 in Dublin, Ireland. He is considered one of the most influential authors of the 20th century.

Question 6

(Opening quote) Edgar Mitchell's essay "From Outer Space to Inner Space" in the anthology he edited, *Psychic Exploration,* p. 35.

"We are in this together..." from *Seeking Jordan,* by Matthew McKay, p. 32.

"Some of these..." from *Seth Speaks*, p. 92.

Reference to Angeles Arrien (1940-2014). Angeles was a shaman, cultural anthropologist, teacher, and an author of several books, including *The Four-Fold Way* and *The Tarot Handbook: Practical Applications of Ancient Visual Symbols*. Above all, she was a person whose life purpose was to encourage others to see their lives in a larger frame. One of her favorite sayings was a quote from the poet Rumi: *"Start a huge, foolish project, like Noah... it makes absolutely no difference what people think of you."* She was a friend to both Frances and Cynthia.

"All the world's a stage..." from *As You Like It*, a play by William Shakespeare.

Reference to Roger Walsh, PhD., who was Frances's life partner for 32 years.

Reference to "hold the circle": Cynthia Spring authored a book titled *Wisdom Circles* (Hyperion, 1998).

DACA—Deferred Action for Childhood Arrivals, a program begun under President Obama for undocumented immigrant children who arrived in the US under the age of 16. The program was put in jeopardy by the Trump administration. Many of the children are now attending college or have full-time work and want to stay in the US. They are referred to as "Dreamers."

(Closing quote) *"I've begun to glimpse..."* from *The Nature of Personal Reality*, by Jane Roberts, p. xi.

Question 7

(Opening quote) from a Ram Dass lecture. Also his latest book is titled: *Walking Each Other Home: Conversations on Loving and Dying.*

"When we leave time..." from *Seeking Jordan*, by Matthew McKay, p. 58.

"Earth is not..." McKay, p. 107.

"Until now, ..." spoken by Andre Luiz, from *The Messengers: Life in the Spirit World*, as channeled by Francisco Xavier, p. 15.

"I relaxed into peace..." spoken by Frances Banks, from *Testimony of Light*, p. 17.

Reference to talk given by Cynthia Spring to a local ecology group in March, 2013, with the title: *We Are Nature Too: One Species Among Many.*

Epilogue

Book One refers to the fact that this book is the first of a trilogy. Book Two is underway (as of Spring, 2019).

Source References

Book references

A Course in Miracles: Text, Workbook and Manual for Teachers, channeled by Helen Schucman, first published by the Foundation for Inner Peace. Mill Valley, CA: 1975.

The Courage to Create, by Rollo May. New York: Bantam Books, 1975.

The Grace in Dying: A Message of Hope, Comfort, and Spiritual Transformation, by Kathleen Dowling Singh. San Francisco: HarperSanFrancisco, 1998.

Heaven and Hell Unveiled: Updates from the World of Spirit, by Stafford Betty. White Crow Books, 2014.

Life After Life, by Raymond Moody, Jr., M.D. New York: Bantam Books, 1975.

Lovingkindness: The Revolutionary Art of Happiness, by Sharon Salzberg and Jon Kabat-Zinn. Boulder, CO: Shambhala, 2002.

Mind Trek: Exploring Consciousness, Time, and Space through Remote Viewing, by Joe McMoneagle and Charles T. Tart. Newburyport, MA: Hampton Roads Publishing, 1993.

One Mind: How Our Individual Mind Is Part of a Greater Consciousness and Why It Matters, by Larry Dossey, M.D. Carlsbad, CA: Hay House, 2013.

Psychic Exploration, an anthology edited by Dr. Edgar Mitchell and John White. Cosimo Books, 2011 (current edition; original edition published in 1974).

Seeking Jordan: How I Learned about Death and the Invisible Universe, by Matthew McKay. Novato, CA: New World Library, 2016.

The Tarot Handbook: Practical Applications of Ancient Visual Symbols, by Angeles Arrien. New York City: Tarcher, 1997.

Testimony of Light: An Extraordinary Message of Life After Death, by Helen Greaves. New York: TarcherPerigee, 2009.

To Heaven and Back: A Doctor's Extraordinary Account of Her Death, Heaven, Angels and Life Again: A True Story, by Dr. Mary Neal. Colorado Springs, CO: WaterBrook, 2012.

Walking Each Other Home: Conversations on Loving and Dying, by Ram Dass and Mirabai Bush. Louisville, CO: Sounds True, 2018.

The Wave and The Drop: Wisdom Stories about Death and Afterlife, by Cindy Spring. El Cerrito, CA: Wisdom Circles Publishing, 2018.

The Way Back to Paradise, by Joseph M. Felser, Ph.D. Charlottesville, VA: Hampton Roads Publishing, 2005.

- **Books by Richard Bach**

  Jonathan Livingston Seagull. London: Macmillan, 1970.

  Illusions: The Adventures of a Reluctant Messiah. New York: Delacorte Press, 1978.

  One: A Novel. New York: Dell, 1989.

  Bridge across Forever. New York: William Morrow, 2006.

- **Books by Robert Monroe**

  Journeys Out of the Body. New York: Doubleday, 1971.

  Far Journeys. New York: Doubleday, 1985.

  Ultimate Journey. New York: Doubleday, 1994.

- **Books by Jane Roberts**

  Seth Speaks: The Eternal Validity of the Soul. San Rafael, CA: Amber-Allen, reprinted 1994.

  The Nature of Personal Reality. San Rafael, CA: Amber-Allen, reprinted 1994.

The Afterdeath Journal of an American Philosopher: The View of William James. Port Washington, NY: New Awareness Network, 2001.

- **Books by Stephan A. Schwartz**

The Alexandria Project. New York: Open Road, 2017 (updated from 1983 edition).

The Secret Vaults of Time: Psychic Archeology and the Quest for Man's Beginnings. Bloomington, IN: iUniverse, 2001.

The Vision: A Novel of Time and Consciousness. Westport, CT: Greenwood Press, 2018. (He uses a fiction format to muse on the kinds of difficulties remote viewers can get into when they can see "ahead of time.")

- **Books by Russell Targ**

Exploring Nonlocal Consciousness and Spiritual Healing. Novato, CA: New World Library, 1999.

The Reality of ESP: A Physicist's Proof of Psychic Realities. Wheaton, IL: Quest Books, 2012.

- **Books by Charles T. Tart, PhD**

Altered States of Consciousness. New York: Doubleday, 1972 (a classic anthology).

Learning to Use Extrasensory Perception. Bloomington, IN: iUniverse, 2001.

The Secret Science of the Soul: How Evidence of the Paranormal Is Bringing Science & Spirit Together. Berkeley, CA: Fearless Books, 2017.

- **Books by Frances Vaughan**

Awakening Intuition. New York: Anchor Books, 1979.

Gifts from A Course in Miracles: Accept This Gift, A Gift of Peace, A Gift of Healing, with Roger Walsh. New York: Tarcher, 1995.

- *Books channeled by Francisco Xavier*

The Messengers: Life in the Spirit World. Conselho Espirita Internacional, 2008 (new edition).

Nosso Lar: Life in the Spirit World. Conselho Espirita Internacional, 2006 (new edition).

YouTube videos

There are hundreds of YouTube videos on topics in this book. Here are a few of my favorite ones. Most of the authors in the **Book Reference** *section can be found in videos and audio programs as well.*

New Thinking Allowed is a video series hosted by psychologist Dr. Jeffrey Mishlove that features many of the people and topics mentioned in this book. *www.youtube.com/channel/UCFk448Yb-GITLnzplK7jwNcw*

Third-Eye Spies with Russell Targ — Targ previews a documentary released in March, 2019 that covers the work at SRI (Stanford Research International) during the 1970s and '80s. SRI worked with excellent remote viewers for the CIA, spying on the Soviet Union during the Cold War. *https://www.youtube.com/watch?v=k9AsG1iNAyc*

Remote Viewing the Future with Stephan A. Schwartz — He discusses a project he was engaged in from 1978 through 1996, asking individuals who attended his workshops and conferences to envision life in the year 2050. He describes the care he took to avoid suggesting answers himself. The results consistently described situations that turned out to be true, but were hard for him to accept at the time — including the disappearance of the Soviet Union. *https://www.youtube.com/watch?v=avbsEEz98Ck*

In other Stephan Schwartz videos on **New Thinking Allowed** he discusses his adventures in underwater archeology and discovering lost ships, including two that belonged to Christopher Columbus.

Six Decades in Parapsychology with Charles T. Tart — This is a great overview by someone considered a master in the field. Dr. Tart has appeared many times on *New Thinking Allowed*. *https://www.youtube.com/watch?v=RVgT3kXjoso*

Jane Roberts was an extraordinary channeler whose work with the entity Seth remains the gold standard in the field. If you go to YouTube and search for Jane Roberts, you will discover a number of black/white grainy interviews with her, as well as actual video of her channeling Seth. *https://www.youtube.com/watch?v=K6RuJ65DvJ0*

See also: *www.sethlearningcenter.org*

Films

Coco (Pixar/Disney, 2017). The film won the Oscar in 2018 for best animated movie. It captures the adventures of Miguel, a Mexican boy who crosses over to "the other side" on the Day of the Dead to enlist his ancestors in helping him become a musician. There are references in the film that you might not have understood if you hadn't read this book.

Ghost (Paramount Pictures, 1990). While out on the town one evening, New York couple Sam (Patrick Swayze) and Molly (Demi Moore) are confronted by a mugger. After submitting to his demands, Sam is murdered anyway. He then finds himself as a disembodied spirit, wandering without hope until he finds another spirit who gives him some helpful pointers on how to co-exist. Sam contacts a psychic (Whoopi Goldberg), and together, the two set out to convince Molly he exists in another dimension and still loves her. Many hilarious scenes. Again, this book will illuminate more of the subtleties of the movie for you.

Third-Eye Spies (Conscious Universe Films, 2019) is a documentary feature film that tells the story of collaboration between researchers into psychic abilities at Stanford Research Institute

(SRI), the CIA, and military intelligence from the early 1970s to the 1990s. Newly declassified documents underscore the stories told by Russell Targ, Stephan Schwartz, Uri Geller, Joe McMoneagle, and others who worked as remote viewers, primarily spying on the Soviet Union. (The Russians had their psychic spies, too.) This documentary shows us that psi abilities can take us beyond the space/time dimension, and can also be weaponized. As Targ states: "The evidence for extra sensory perception is overwhelming and shows a talent we all share and deserve to know about."

Meeting others who share this interest

Who can we share this with? Who among family and friends will join us in conversations about this greater reality? It's obvious that speaking from experience is much better than speaking from simply an intellectual understanding, or even a belief system. Even if there are at least 13 million people in the U.S. (as estimated by a 1980 Gallup poll) who have had near-death experiences that included a visit to a strange and beautiful world, very few of them talk about it openly. There are many NDE support groups that meet in private, but members need to have had a verifiable NDE to join. (Not a credential one cares to obtain.)

Organizations for further inquiry

International Association for Near-Death Studies (IANDS) focuses most of its resources on providing quality information available about NDE-related subjects. It is the only such membership group in the world. In addition to maintaining a website (*https://iands.org*), IANDS publishes a peer-reviewed scholarly journal and a member magazine, sponsors conferences and other programs, works with the media, and encourages the formation of regional discussion and support groups.

Institute for Noetic Studies (IONS) is a nonprofit organization dedicated to supporting individual and collective transformation through consciousness research, transformative learning, and engaging a global community in the realization of our human

potential. Their goal is to create a shift in consciousness world-
wide — where people recognize that we are all part of an inter-
connected whole and are inspired to take action to help humanity
and the planet thrive. *https://ions.org*

Raymond Moody's University of Heaven website, *https://
theuniversityofheaven.com,* is an online educational platform committed to offering quality courses and resources about near-death,
shared-death, and after-death experiences. The website is curated
by Dr. Raymond Moody with his colleague Lisa Smartt.

Psychic abilities:

Telepathy means sending and receiving messages non-verbally through mind-to-mind connection. (See books by Charles T. Tart)

Clairvoyance is also known as remote viewing. (See Glossary)

Psychic healing takes place when a person is freed from disease or an ailment and restored to health by psychic or spiritual means.

Psychokinesis is the ability to affect or move physical objects by mental effort alone. Israeli psychic Uri Geller many times demonstrated his ability to bend spoons at a distance.

Precognition is the successful prediction of future events when such events couldn't be rationally predicted.

Mediumship refers to connecting an incarnate person with someone on the other side, often a loved one.

Channeling. (See Glossary)

Automatic writing. (See Glossary)

Instrumental Transcommunication (ITC) refers to methods using audio or video equipment that demonstrate communication with discarnate beings, usually deceased persons. Computers and telephones have also have been sources of messages from the other side.

Meditation refers to many techniques from religious and secular sources that offer how to train the mind in focus, calmness, clarity, and freedom from thoughts.

Dowsing has become more than looking for water with a divining rod. It includes looking for water, minerals, metals, and lost objects using paranormal abilities. (See American Society of Dowsers at *https://dowsers.org*)

Out-of-Body travel (OBE). (See Glossary)

Near-Death experience (NDE). (See Glossary)

Shared-death experience (SDE) is a term coined by Dr. Raymond Moody to describe experiences where bystanders who are close to a dying person experience many of the same aspects of the NDE along with the dying person, including leaving their bodies, meeting beings of light, and seeing the life review of the dying person. These bystanders are themselves healthy and not dying, yet seem to share these experiences. *https://www.near-death.com/science/experts/raymond-moody.html*

Connecting with spirit guides. (See Frances's suggestions on p. 51.)

Divination tools:

Tarot. (See Glossary)

Astrology is the study of the movements and relative positions of celestial bodies interpreted as having an influence on human affairs and the natural world.

I Ching. (See Endnotes for Question 4)

Physical portals:

Yoga, hallucinogenic drugs, sweat lodges, whirling (a Sufi form of spiritual practice); possibly, death-defying activities such as mountain climbing, deep-sea diving, or landing on the moon.

Daily experiences:

Heightened sensory awareness, elasticity of time, synchronicity clusters, fairy helpers (for example, for parking spaces)

Traditional Gateways:

Art, music and poetry — whether created by others or your own creations

Spending time out-of-doors

Unconventional ways to a greater awareness: Working in or volunteering for:

Homeless shelters

Refugee camps

War zones

Children's cancer wards

Animal shelters

FOOD FOR THOUGHT

Throughout her communication with us, Frances offers gems of insight. For me, they are ways to evoke new levels of understanding. I've chosen one from each chapter. This is another portal to the greater reality for your consideration. Here is the basic practice:

- Eyes open, deep breaths.
- Close eyes, check in with your environment (contact, sounds, smells).
- Scan body.
- Focus on breath.
- Ask yourself the question.
- Back to breath.
- Ask yourself the question again, but as if for the first time.
- Back to breath. (and so on)

Here are the lines I have chosen from Frances:

"We each put on a persona, one for each lifetime. Some of us have enormous closets full. But we love each one for its courage, and perseverance, and mistakes that helped all of us in our soul group learn from."

Question for contemplation: What am I learning from my current persona?

"You and I are blending our minds and souls together to produce this book. It's not one or the other of us. Neither could do this on her own. It's another example of Communion."

Question for contemplation: Who is giving me help from the other side?

"When I prayed I knew I was both supplicant and recipient of the prayer as part of the Whole."

Question for contemplation: When I pray, or ask for help from the greater reality, am I including myself as the recipient of the request?

"Once you start trusting [intuition], you'll be turning to it more often. Then you'll begin to wonder where those answers are coming from. Then you're in inquiry mode and it will lead you to broader vistas and ways of knowing."

Question for contemplation: Do I trust my intuition?

"There are so many more dimensions of reality than even our most fertile minds on earth can imagine. Suffice it to say that we are complex beings in toto, leading singular lives across a spectrum of time and places."

Question for contemplation: Do I ever get a glimpse of another lifetime I'm living?

"Remember Angeles's wonderful questions: What's learnin' ya today? What's workin' ya? In other words, what's the teacher [in life] that's confronting you today?"

Question for contemplation: What's learnin' me today?

"You may have chosen a humble garb for this incarnation, but don't be fooled! You are divine — a part of a timeless and limitless expanse of being with many other aspects to yourself not part of your earthly person, but nonetheless a greater being who let out a shard of itself into the dense

matter of earth for a learning, a chance to create something unique for all of us."

Question for contemplation: What is my unique contribution for this lifetime?

A Closing Story of How Immensity Happens

If a chessboard were to have a grain of wheat placed upon each square such that one grain were placed on the first square, two on the second, four on the third, and so on (doubling the number of grains on each subsequent square), how many grains of wheat would be on the last square of the chessboard at the finish?

The problem may be solved using simple addition. With 64 squares on a chessboard, if the number of grains doubles on successive squares, then the sum of grains on all 64 squares is: $1 + 2 + 4 + 8 + ...$ and so forth for the 64 squares. The total number of grains on the entire board then equals **18,446,744,073,709,551,615**, much higher than most expect. On the 64th square of the chessboard alone there would be $2^{63} = 9,223,372,036,854,775,808$ grains. This number exceeds the total number of atoms in the sun.

DEEP GRATITUDE TO...

Frances Vaughan, who chose me to be a channel for her ongoing work in bringing a message of Love and Light to our darkening world.

Charlie Garfield, my soulmate of 38 years (in this lifetime) who supports me in every way. When I got "wobbly" from transiting dimensions, he was there to say "Let's talk." When I wanted to watch YouTube videos on psychic development instead of the latest movie, he said, "OK." And most of all, when I had to "come out of the closet" as a channel for Frances and all that implies, he stood by me and smiled.

Dan Drasin, a special friend of almost 40 years. As far back as 1981 he introduced me to sources of wisdom from the greater reality. More recently, he has kept me abreast of advances in parapsychology. For the past three years he has been my personal mentor in gaining perspective on "the big picture," always recommending the best resources for the next step in my journey.

Regina Ochoa, an extraordinary medium whose experiences in the greater reality have impressed and informed thousands of people. Yet she found time to advise and comfort me when I was receiving my first telepathic messages and didn't know which way was up. Given her depth of knowledge, her response to her first reading of *Seven Questions* was crucial to my knowing that I was on the right track. It was, "WOW!"

Matthew McKay, whose talk in January, 2018 about contacting his son Jordan inspired me to try automatic writing. It worked and here we are. Your work is healing for many.

Ellen Jones-Walker, consciousness educator and my teacher at the week-long Gateway program I took at The Monroe Institute near Charlottesville, VA. Her manner of support and openness to any kind of question made me feel I was in the right place, despite how much more experienced most of my classmates were. She also exuded a certainty about the existence of the greater reality better than any words could convey. (Many thanks also, for copy editing an early draft, and raising questions that helped me clarify the message.)

I would not have been able to enter this unknown (to me) territory without the love and support of my friends and manuscript reviewers, many of whom had never before read channeled writings. Elisabeth Belle, Judith Frank, Shelli Fried, Patti Hamel, Bharat Lindemood, Clarice Moussalli, and Mimi Zemmelman.

To my production team: Naomi Rose, outstanding self-publishing consultant and a superb editor besides, Margaret Copeland, cover and interior designer who has worked her magic again, Gabriel Steinfeld, excellent proofreader who actually enjoys nitpicking semi-colons, and Matthew Simmons, our creative webmaster. (Any unconventional punctuation and grammar decisions are entirely made by author.)

To the testimonial givers: Matthew McKay, Ellen Jones-Walker, Regina Ochoa, Lisa Smartt: I am grateful for your tributes and ongoing support.

PERMISSIONS

About the Authors

 **Frances Vaughan** was a psychologist and teacher who inspired everyone she met to be his or her higher self. She wrote books and papers that carried on the wisdom and compassion that she has gathered from many lifetimes. She served as a trustee for 19 years at the Fetzer Institute, which helps build a spiritual foundation for a loving world. As a transpersonal psychotherapist she helped guide her clients to find the source of their healing. She continues her work through this book collaboration.

"Frances was a respected 'Wise Woman' and a true elder. She embodied the strong feminine and was a model of an extraordinarily bright mind meeting an ever expanding heart."

— FRANK OSTASESKI, Founder of Metta Institute, author of *The Five Invitations: Discovering What Death Can Teach Us About Living Fully*

Books: *Awakening Intuition* (Anchor Books, 1979), *The Inward Arc: Healing in Psychotherapy and Spirituality* (iUniverse, 2001) and *Shadows of the Sacred: Seeing Through Spiritual Illusions* (Quest Books, 1995). With her husband, Roger Walsh, she is co-editor of *Paths Beyond Ego: The Transpersonal Vision* (Tarcher, 1993) and *Gifts from A Course in Miracles,* including *Accept this Gift, A Gift of Peace and A Gift of Healing* (Tarcher, 1995). Published separately and as one volume. *www.francesvaughan.com*

Cynthia Spring is an author, social activist, and explorer of the unconventional. Since the mid 1990s, she has been active in local ecology in the San Francisco area. She co-founded two ecology nonprofits, Earth-Team and Close to Home, as well as serving as coordinator for Earth Day 2000 for the Bay Area. Her explorations have been in the fields of spirituality, transpersonal psychology and personal growth. She lives in Northern California with her husband Charlie, and two cats, Bella and Layla.

Books: *The Wave and The Drop: Wisdom Stories about Death and Afterlife* (Wisdom Circles Publishing, 2018), and *Wisdom Circles: A Guide to Self-Discovery and Community Building in Small Groups* (Hyperion, 1998). She co-authored *Sometimes My Heart Goes Numb: Love and Caregiving in a Time of AIDS* with Charles Garfield (Jossey-Bass 1995). She co-edited the anthology *Earthlight: Spiritual Wisdom for an Ecological Age* (2007). She was also the producer (1981-1996) of over 100 nonfiction audiobooks. See *https://cindyspring.com*